The Oral History Manual

The Oral History Manual

Second Edition

Barbara W. Sommer and
Mary Kay Quinlan

AltaMira
PRESS

A Division of
ROWMAN & LITTLEFIELD PUBLISHERS, INC.

Lanham • New York • Toronto • Plymouth, UK

AltaMira Press
A division of Rowman & Littlefield Publishers, Inc.
A wholly owned subsidiary of The Rowman & Littlefield Publishing Group, Inc.
4501 Forbes Boulevard, Suite 200
Lanham, MD 20706
www.altamirapress.com

Estover Road
Plymouth PL6 7PY
United Kingdom

British Library Cataloguing in Publication Information Available

Library of Congress Cataloging-in-Publication Data
Sommer, Barbara W.
 The oral history manual / Barbara W. Sommer and Mary Kay Quinlan. — 2nd ed.
   p. cm.
 Includes bibliographical references and index.
 ISBN 978-0-7591-1157-8 (cloth : alk. paper) — ISBN 978-0-7591-1158-5 (pbk. : alk. paper) — ISBN 978-0-7591-1805-8 (electronic)
 1. Oral history—Handbooks, manuals, etc. 2. Oral History—Methodology. 3. Interviewing—Handbooks, manuals, etc.
4. Historiography. I. Quinlan, Mary Kay. II. Title.

D16.14.S69 2009
907.2—dc22   2008051514

Printed in the United States of America

Contents

Remember the time Grandma burned the Thanksgiving turkey? I think it was the only time we had an all-vegetarian turkey-day dinner.

I'll never forget that horrible day, how devastated I was when the auctioneer came to sell the farm. Four generations it had been in our family. I felt like I'd betrayed them all.

Back then, there was probably maybe six or seven colored people working in this plant, that was probably total. . . . You could count them on one hand and one finger on the other.

Stories are the fabric of our lives. Stories about families and jobs and neighborhoods and institutions and ethnic groups and social movements. Stories of people and the places that matter to them, both far away and close to home. Hilarious stories. Tragic stories. Matter-of-fact stories. Setting-the-record-straight stories.

Oral history can collect all of those kinds of stories and more because it is a special kind of story collecting. It's a process that goes beyond putting a recorder in the middle of the table at a family reunion and pressing the "start" button or asking elderly folks in the community to reminisce about the olden days. An anecdote from Grandma's girlhood, an oft-told tale of wartime heroism, a gut-wrenching memory of racial hatred—all of these can be the beginnings of an oral account of a past time or place. But standing alone, these nuggets from the past are just beginnings.

Often, however, they inspire people to embark on a systematic effort to go beyond the stand-alone, individual experience and explore the story and its meanings more thoroughly. Do other people recall similar experiences? Or different ones? How are the stories from people's memories the same as or different from what's already on the record about a particular subject? This manual will show you how to pursue an oral history project that will stand the test of time by going beyond the collection of isolated personal tales. Like the first edition of *The Oral History Manual,* this edition is predicated on the notion that the knowledge locked in people's memories can add vital information

and unique human perspectives to our collective understanding of the past. Documenting that information in a systematic way adds value to the storehouse of human knowledge.

Indeed, in the United States alone, well-crafted oral history projects in recent years have documented the experiences of Tongan immigrants in Utah, Hmong and Tibetan immigrants in Minnesota and Germans from Russia in North Dakota. Other projects have focused on industrial history—a pulp mill in Washington State, a scooter factory in Nebraska, a nuclear weapons plant in Colorado. Still others explore the lives of individuals—artists with disabilities, World War II army nurses, members of Congress, presidential aides, retired FBI agents, civil rights activists. The array of contemporary oral history projects blankets virtually every imaginable theme in the broadest sense of modern political and social history.

This edition of *The Oral History Manual,* like its predecessor, details the fundamentals of conceptualizing, planning, and carrying out an oral history project. In addition, users of this edition will find:

- an expanded discussion of project budgeting,
- more information on legal and ethical considerations, particularly those that affect oral history work in academic settings,
- an updated section on selecting oral history recording equipment;
- a discussion of cross-cultural interviewing considerations; and
- updated recommendations on processing oral history materials.

Just as a successful oral history project is inevitably the product of many contributors, so also is this manual. We are indebted to our oral history mentors and the countless oral historians and would-be oral historians we have encountered by teaching college-level classes and community workshops and attending professional conferences over many years. They have challenged us to articulate our convictions about the importance of adhering to standard practices in carrying out oral history projects, and they have inspired us with the dedication, enthusiasm, and creativity they bring to the process.

Among others, we wish to thank: Susan Becker, Doug Boyd, James E. Fogerty, Karen Gerrity, Thomas Saylor, and John Wolford for their thoughtful critiques of all or part of this edition. And we are indebted to Martha Ross, Donald A. Ritchie, and John A. Neuenschwander for their ongoing support and inspiration and to the late Willa Baum for her leadership and energy in promoting the careful practice of oral history.

We hope you enjoy your oral history adventure. Many years from now you may remember the exact words, tone of voice, and facial expression a narrator used in answering a question only you thought to ask. And you can take satisfaction in knowing that your effort has preserved that story—a piece of the fabric of history that gives meaning to all our lives.

CHAPTER 1

Introduction to Oral History

In June 1944, when United States Army historian Forrest C. Pogue picked up a wire recorder on a hospital ship off Omaha Beach and began doing interviews with soldiers wounded in D-Day battles, he may not have been thinking of oral history. Although he was collecting first-person information, the term had yet to be formally applied to the methodology.[1] But his work, done under the direction of chief army historian S. L. A. Marshall, helped lay the groundwork for the development of oral history as a research technique.[2] Oral History in the Mid-Atlantic Region (OHMAR) now has an annual award in his name that recognizes outstanding and continuing contributions to the field.

WHAT IS ORAL HISTORY?

What do you think when you hear the words "oral history"? Many define oral history as spoken stories about things that happened in the past. But confusion creeps in when we begin to examine the definition. Are family reminiscences oral history? What about oral traditions? Or journalists' stories about past events? What is the difference between each of these types of narratives and oral history? Is there a difference? Yes, there is, and this manual will help you learn about those differences and how to master oral history methodology.

> Oral history is primary-source material created in an interview setting with a witness to or a participant in an event or a way of life for the purpose of preserving the information and making it available to others. The term refers both to the process and the interview itself.

So what is oral history and how did this term come to be applied to the collection of first-person information? In 1980 and 1984, Charles T. Morrissey wrote articles published in *The Oral History Review* describing the origins of the term.[3] What is "oral" and what is "history," and when the words are used together, what exactly does "oral history" mean? He concluded that, although it is a generic term that may be interpreted in a variety of ways, it refers to a basic structured collection of spoken firsthand memories in an interview setting. Since the introduction of oral history as a name for the spoken memory interviews that Allen Nevins began collecting at Columbia University in the late 1940s the term has been identified with the process of collecting oral information about the past.

Because the spoken firsthand memories given in an interview are from a witness to or a participant in an event or time period, they are primary-source material, "the material by which history is known."[4] In previous times, information collected by oral historians may only have been part of a written record such as letters, diaries, or other "substantive and meaningful documents."[5]

In the years since the term first began to be used, oral history has come to have a popular (vernacular) and an archival meaning.[6] The archival meaning is more precise and is based on the use of standard methodology as defined by several key elements:

> The key elements of oral history are the essential framework that guides oral history practitioners.

- Careful attention to copyright and other legal and ethical issues
- A structured, well-researched interview format
- A controlled, recorded interview setting
- Collection of firsthand information
- Probing follow-up questions that seek depth and detail
- Use of high-quality recording equipment
- Adherence to careful processing techniques
- Provisions for making the interviews available to others at an accessible repository

Willa Baum summed up the importance of these key elements and standard methodology when she said: "The goal is a good historical account, first-hand, preserved, and available."[7]

Oral history interviews are grouped into two categories: life interviews and project interviews. Life interviews involve multiple interview sessions with one person to create a collection of autobiographical materials. Oral history projects encompass a series of interviews with a variety of individuals about a specific historical topic, place, or event of interest. Projects can be one-time tasks or ongoing, multi-year activities that regularly add a small number of interviews. In either case, care in planning and adherence to oral history process help support interviews that have depth and nuance.

Who participates in an oral history interview? The interviewer develops the interview structure. This includes helping with background research, developing questions, scheduling the interview, conducting the interview, and taking care of follow-up tasks. The narrator is chosen for his or her firsthand knowledge about the interview topic and the ability to communicate this information.

NEW FACTORS IN ORAL HISTORY

The use of oral history has grown considerably in size and sophistication since its World War II and post–World War II beginnings. Aided by the relatively recent definition of the field of public history and the increased interest in history from the bottom up—social history of non-elites—that began in the 1960s, the collection of new historical sources in the form of first-person information has become an active outreach effort throughout the world. Along the way, as the collection and use of oral history has expanded, it has faced some major developments that have helped further define it. Outlined by Alistair Thomson in a 2007 issue of *The Oral History Review*, they include:

- Increased understanding of the importance of memory as "people's history"
- Clarification of an understanding of the "subjectivity" of memory
- Discussion about the role of the oral historian as interviewer
- The impact of technology through the digital revolution

Serving as a backdrop to the new developments, several other factors have had an influence on oral history. These are:

- The growing significance of political and legal practices in which personal testimony is used as a central resource
- The increase in interdisciplinary approaches to interviewing
- The proliferation of studies relating to history and memory
- The evolving internationalism of oral history[8]

These points, which trace oral history's evolution, emphasize the importance of understanding methodology and its impact on defining interview context and content.

ORAL HISTORY AND OTHER FORMS OF RECORDED FIRST-PERSON INFORMATION

Oral history shares key elements with other first-person collecting techniques. This brings to mind again the generic basis of the term. What are some of the differences and why are they important? Each collecting technique is discipline-based and adheres to the standards of its discipline. While all collect valuable information about the past, research preparation, interviewing techniques, and copyright control may vary. For instance, oral history and folklore are closely related and are described as being on "opposite ends of a continuum."[9] But the information collected through oral history and folklore interviews can have subtle differences. Folklorists work with genres—traditional songs, stories, and other information, fact or fiction—as well as in historical information.[10] Interviewing techniques also may vary. Donald A. Ritchie provided an example: "An oral historian would most likely interview a husband and wife separately, seeking to identify the unique perspective of each spouse. A folklorist, being as interested in the way a story is told as in its substance, would interview the couple together to observe the interplay as one begins a story and the other finishes it."[11]

People sometimes think of journalistic interviews about historical topics as oral history. Here differences can include the purpose for which the materials are collected, their immediate intended use, control of copyright, and plans made for disposition and long-term availability of original interview materials. The purpose of journalism is to collect, write, and publish the news. The journalistic sound bite is not part of the oral history process. Oral historians use and benefit from journalistic techniques but the key elements in oral history methodology set it apart from journalism.

Many academic historians whose work focuses on 20th- and 21st-century history conduct interviews as part of their research. Often, historians call such research oral history. But unless their narrators have signed donor forms and the interviews are somehow available to others, such interviews do not, strictly speaking, meet the standard definition of oral history.

Linda Shopes noted another difference. Writing for the Oral History Association's Mellon Project Committee, she described "personal experience stories"[12] that register "a certain democratic or populist meaning." StoryCorps, with a "rekindling [of] interest in the storied quality of everyday life," is an example of this popular, sometimes called vernacular, interviewing technique. Contrasting with the vernacular, Shopes wrote of the "more precise, bounded meaning" of oral history used by scholars.[13] Although personal experience stories often are compelling, the interviews are not always oral history. The key elements that emphasize careful planning and objective inquiry define oral history.

Oral historians sometimes refer to oral traditions, the transfer of information handed down orally from generation to generation, when discussing the use of memory to document history. Describing this transfer of knowledge, Blackfeet storyteller and musician Jack Gladstone calls oral traditions "living stories." Collection and use of oral traditions continues today, primarily among indigenous people. But as William Schneider, Melissa K. Nelson, and others have noted, the recording and use of recorded oral traditions can differ from oral history. Oral traditions, though they may be told in the first person, can represent centuries-old stories. Sometimes they include sacred or culturally sensitive information and often there are traditional protocols or rules for their telling and use. While all oral history practitioners understand the importance of documenting interview content and context, identifying how, where, when, and why a recording of oral traditions was made; how, when, where, and why the recording is and will continue to be used—orally and in writing—and how, where, when, and why the traditional stories will continue to be told, is part of understanding the impact of oral culture on the recording of these living stories.[14]

Oral history is sometimes confused with recorded speeches or with someone reading historical documents into a recorder. This is not oral history. Audio or video reminiscences collected by turning on a recorder and asking Grandma to talk about the olden days or recording conversations at family reunions also are often confused with oral history.[15]

What, then, is oral history? Oral history is characterized by a structured, systematic planning process, thorough research, careful consideration of copyright, emphasis on depth and detail of information collected, and adherence to strict processing techniques. Oral history, despite the generic use of the term, is a research methodology with a "precise, bounded meaning" and a process that supports and defines the interview as the active collecting step.

> Oral history is a research methodology with a clear and defined process that supports the interview as the active collecting step.

HOW IS ORAL HISTORY USED?

The use of oral history often goes beyond the original collecting scope, giving it a potential for wide applicability. Oral history does much more than document new information. It provides all those who use it a window to the past and, in doing so, makes history come alive. It reminds us that the actors are real people, each with a unique perspective on the past and present. It helps us understand not just what happened, but how those telling the story understood what happened and what they may now think of it. Exploring many sides of an issue through multiple first-hand individual accounts offers the opportunity to uncover layers of meaning embedded in the stories and insights into how people understand and interpret the past and their place in it. These examples represent a few of its many uses:

Oral history projects help document events in the history of a community. Life interviews, created for family or genealogical purposes, also can be used as community history sources. Although local in focus, the contributions of community-based interviews to greater understanding of related state, national, and international issues should not be overlooked. They can contain valuable information that goes beyond their original purpose. In one Great Plains community, an oral history project that documented responses to race relations, missile locations during the Cold War, upheaval in the farm economy, and changes in people's perceptions of Main Street, while important to an understanding of the community itself, provided invaluable grassroots insight into issues of national importance.

Oral history serves people with a history of disenfranchisement. Those with little or no written record, or for whom the written record is distorted at best, benefit greatly from the use of oral history. Oral history is inclusive, bringing in many voices, not just the more powerful or dominant that are traditionally included in existing records. Oral historians look at their work as a way to complement and supplement the existing record, as well as a chance to make fundamental changes or additions to it. In many cases, while documenting the community's history is critical in itself, an oral history project or a set of life interviews can become a catalyst. It can provide an avenue to correct long-held misconceptions about an event or a time period, help collect information that balances the existing record, and become an impetus for developing community pride through the telling of people's stories in their own words.

Oral history can help preserve languages and dialects. By preserving the sound and cadence of spoken words, it can help keep languages alive. It is used as a tool to save the vernacular or, in the case of American Indians, rapidly vanishing languages.

Oral history is used in the classroom as a teaching technique. Its interdisciplinary nature, drawing on a variety of research, verbal, writing, and technical skills, and its built-in ability to tie the school to the community bring a unique focus and skill set to a curriculum.[16]

Oral history, with its emphasis on personal outreach, can help benefit an entire community by bringing people together—narrators with interviewers and others interested in the work of the project. Regardless of the role it plays in community organization, it can become a vehicle for documenting not only facts about the past but also more subjective insights into how people organize their views of their history and how their frames of reference in their own communities affect their firsthand spoken memories of the events discussed in an interview.

PROCESS MATTERS

Do you need to hold a Ph.D. in history to do oral history? No, definitely not. Is a thorough understanding of the methodology important to the collection of substantive oral history? Yes, it is—not just to those who collect the information but to those who will use it. David Henige wrote in 1986: "Some of those who collect oral histories may not think of themselves as historians because they have no intention of using those tapes in historical reconstructions. . . . Whatever their goals, they *are* providing historical sources, and no historian's work can be better than his or her sources. All such collectors, then, have the obligation, and hopefully the desire, to be as concerned with methodologi-

cal issues as are those who will use the tapes."[17] Francis Good echoed these comments two decades later, in 2007: "A scholarly understanding of what constitutes good practice is essential not just for practitioners, but also for critical evaluation of oral sources, where these contribute to scholarly insight through evaluation and interpretation of their evidence."[18]

Oral history represents one of many ways to document the past. It brings an immediacy and an ability to explore subjective nuances to a study of the past. It allows researchers to probe beneath the surface of the written record to discover not just what happened but how and why, to explain anomalies, to provide convincing evidence or tantalizing clues that enhance understanding of a past time and place. Through it, information that otherwise might have been lost can be collected and preserved as primary-source material for researchers. And it can help pass a sense of the richness of the human experience to future generations. Moreover, a well-planned and well-executed oral history project can bring people together as they collectively work to understand more about the past.

The following pages take the reader through a detailed, step-by-step approach to doing oral history. They explain what works and why. And if you get hooked on oral history—as untold numbers of people have—it offers resources for more ideas on creating and using oral histories. Each chapter is devoted to a specific topic, beginning with an overview of oral history methodology steps, and then moving to a discussion of planning steps, legal and ethical issues, equipment and technology issues, interview preparation, interviewing guidelines, and processing guidelines. The appendices contain sample forms, a list of selected readings, and a reprint of the Oral History Association Evaluation Guidelines, the statement of professional standards governing the collection and use of oral history.

NOTES

1. Charles T. Morrissey described the adoption of the term by the Columbia University program in "Why Call It 'Oral History'? Searching for Early Usage of a Generic Term." *The Oral History Review* (1980):20–48.

2. Donald A. Ritchie, "Remembering Forrest Pogue," *Oral History Association Newsletter*, Winter 1997:7.

3. See Morrissey, "Why Call It 'Oral History?" and Charles T. Morrissey, "Riding a Mule through the 'Terminological Jungle': Oral History and Problems of Nomenclature," *The Oral History Review* 12 (1984):13–28.

4. Carol Kammen and Norma Prendergast, eds., *Encyclopedia of Local History* (Walnut Creek, CA: AltaMira Press, 2000):383.

5. Kammen and Prendergast, *Encyclopedia of Local History*:357.

6. For more information, see Linda Shopes, "Background Paper: Oral History," Oral History Association, http://alpha.dickinson.edu/oha/pdf/Mellon%20Position%20Report.pdf, accessed February 7, 2008.

7. Willa Baum, "The Other Uses of Oral History," *The Oral History Review* 34:1 (Winter/Spring 2007):15.

8. Alistair Thomson, "Four Paradigm Transformations in Oral History," *The Oral History Review* 34:1 (Winter/Spring 2007):49–70. For more information, see Paul Thompson, *The Voice of the Past: Oral History,* 3rd ed. (New York, NY: Oxford University Press, 2000). Valerie Raleigh Yow, *Recording Oral History: A Guide for the Humanities and Social Sciences,* 2nd ed. (Walnut Creek, CA: AltaMira Press, 2005). Michael A. Frisch, *A Shared Authority: Essays on the Craft and Meaning of Oral History and Public History* (Albany, NY: State University of New York Press, 1990). Alessandro Portelli, *The Death of Luigi Trastulli and Other Stories: Form and Meaning in Oral History* (Albany, NY: State University of New York Press, 1991). Ronald J. Grele, *Envelopes of Sound: The Art of Oral History,* 2nd ed. (New York, NY: Praeger Publishers, 1991). Tamara Hareven, "The Search for Generational Memory," in *Oral History: An Interdisciplinary Anthology,* 2nd ed., David K. Dunaway and Willa K. Baum, eds. (Walnut Creek, CA: AltaMira Press, 1996):241–256. David Henige, "Where Seldom Is Heard a Discouraging Word: Method in Oral History," *The Oral History Review* 14 (1986):35–42.

9. Donald A. Ritchie, *Doing Oral History: A Practical Guide,* 2nd ed. (New York, NY: Oxford University Press, 2003):37.

10. Gwen Meister and Barbara W. Sommer, "Oral History Interviewing and Folklore Fieldwork: A Guide for Participants in the Veterans History Project of the American Folklife Center—Library of Congress," PowerPoint presentation, September 11, 2006, slide 6.

11. Ritchie, *Doing Oral History: A Practical Guide*:37.

12. Sandra K. Dolby has identified personal experience stories as a folklore genre. See Mary Ellen Brown and Bruce Rosenberg, eds., *Encyclopedia of Folklore and Literature,* (Denver: ABC-CLIO, 1998), "Personal Experience Story": 504–506, and Jan Harold Bruvand, ed., *American Folklore: An Encyclopedia* (New York: Grand Publishing, 1996), "Personal Experience Story":556–558. See also Linda Shopes, "Making Sense of Oral History: How Do Historians Use It?" in *History Matters: The U.S. Survey Course on the Web,* http://historymatters.gmu.edu/use/oral/how.html, accessed September 29, 2008.

13. Linda Shopes, "Background Paper: Oral History," Oral History Association, http://alpha.dickinson.edu/oha/pdf/Mellon%20Position%20Report.pdf, accessed February 7, 2008:1–2.

14. For more information, see William Schneider, "Sorting Out Oral Tradition and Oral History" in *. . . so they understand: Cultural Issues in Oral History* (Logan, UT: Utah State University Press, 2002):53–66. Julie Cruikshank, *The Social Life of Stories: Narrative and Knowledge in the Yukon Territory* (Lincoln, NE: University of Nebraska Press, 1998). *A Guide for Oral History in the Native American Community,* 3rd ed. developed by the Suquamish Tribal Oral History Project, Suquamish Tribal Cultural Center, Port Madison Indian Reservation, 2000. The Hopi Oral History Project, http://www.nau.edu/hcpo/projects/oralhist.htm, accessed January 7, 2008. Devon A. Mihesuah, "Voices, Interpretations, and the 'New Indian History': Comment on the *American Indian Quarterly*'s Special Issue on Writing about American Indians," *American Indian Quarterly* 20:1 (Winter 1996):91–108. See also Charles E. Trimble, Barbara W. Sommer, and Mary Kay Quinlan, *The American Indian Oral History Manual: Making Many Voices Heard* (Walnut Creek, CA: Left Coast Press, Inc., 2008).

15. For additional information, see "Capturing the Living Past: An Oral History Primer" on the Nebraska State Historical Society website, http://www.nebraskahistory.org/lib-arch/research/audiovis/oral_history, accessed February 7, 2008.

16. For more information, see Glenn Whitman, *Dialogue with the Past: Engaging Students and Meeting Standards through Oral History* (Walnut Creek, CA: AltaMira Press, 2004) and Barry A. Lanman and Laura M. Wendling, *Preparing the Next Generation of Oral Historians: An Anthology of Oral History Education* (Lanham, MD: AltaMira Press, 2006).

17. David Henige, "Where Seldom Is Heard a Discouraging Word: Method in Oral History," *The Oral History Review* 14 (1986):42.

18. Francis Good, "Oral History As Scholarship," H-Oralhist. http://h-net.msu.edu/cgi-bin/logbrowse, May 14, 2007, accessed May 14, 2007.

CHAPTER 2

Planning Overview

The oral history process is a series of steps that results in a primary-source document. The steps are divided into several groups that are summarized below and discussed in detail in the following chapters. Although presented here in the context of an oral history project, they apply equally to the recording of individual interviews.

> Oral history methodology encompasses a series of process steps that support and focus the interview and make it available to users.

ORAL HISTORY PROCESS

Oral history process steps are the building blocks of oral history. The oral history process begins with planning steps that identify strategies, set goals, outline tasks, and formulate a course of action. They lay the basis for doing interviews that have the nuance and depth of oral history. While it may be tempting to skip them and go straight to the interviews, coordinators and leaders will find that, by working through these steps, interviews often have a clearer focus and more prepared and confident interviewers. They also lay the groundwork for maintaining access to the interview information. Planning steps are covered in Chapter Three.

Budget information helps determine real costs, even if a project is relying on volunteers. Organizing a budget also can serve as a guide to help develop grant requests to various funding sources. Budget information and funding sources also are covered in Chapter Three.

Legal and ethical issues are among the most important for oral history practitioners. They provide the basis for the trust relationship between narrator and interviewer that is basic to oral history. They also define the process for current and future accessibility of oral history interview information and guide the work of planners, interviewers, and other project personnel. Chapter Four provides information about legal and ethical issues in oral history.

Equipment decisions also are important for oral history practitioners and are some of the most discussed aspects of oral history project work. Making good decisions about the equipment to use, especially in a time of rapid technological advances, results in more than ending up with a recording that has good sound or video at the time of the interview. These decisions help determine the full range of potential uses of the recording as well as its future retrievability— basic considerations of oral history practitioners. Equipment decisions are covered in Chapter Five.

Interview preparation is a critical part of the oral history process. In addition to developing and focusing interview content, it provides a structure for documenting the context of the interview information. Interviews are the products of an exchange between the narrator and interviewer; oral history theory identifies both as creators of the interview. Careful documentation of decisions about what the interviewer and narrator discussed helps provide a framework for use, present and future, of the spoken memories in the oral history interview. Interview preparation is covered in Chapter Six.

The interview is the outreach, collecting step in the oral history process. During the interview, the interviewer and narrator collaborate to document the narrator's experiences and memories. While the interview is the best-known step, it does not exist in a vacuum. All the steps preceding it and following it are equally important. Conducting the interview is covered in Chapter Seven.

Processing steps follow the interview. They cover housekeeping details to make sure the recordings and interview information are maintained and made accessible to the public according to the best standards of oral history methodology. Processing steps, including preparing materials for ongoing curatorial care, are covered in Chapter Eight.[*]

---

[*] For detailed information on curatorial care of oral history materials, see Nancy MacKay, *Oral Histories: From Interview to Archive* (Walnut Grove, CA: Left Coast Press, 2007).

A list of oral history process steps is given below.

Planning Process Steps
- Identify project leaders and personnel
- Name the project
- Write a mission statement
- Decide who will own the project materials
- Select a project advisory board
- Establish a time frame for completing the project
- Establish record-keeping procedures
- Develop a publicity plan
- Train interviewers

Budget Steps
- Develop a project budget
- Find financial support and funding sources

Legal and Ethical Steps
- Identify legal issues
- Observe ethical standards

Equipment Steps
- Decide on recording equipment and media
- Decide on microphones, cables, and other interview recording needs
- Decide on transcribing equipment

Interview Preparation Steps
- Begin background research and develop a bibliography
- Use the research to create an outline relating to the interview topic
- Make a list of the themes or topics to pursue in the interview
- Identify potential narrators and determine the topics or themes to be covered in interviews with each of them
- Conduct narrator-specific research
- Develop the interview outline
- Schedule the interview

The Interview
- Conduct the interview
- Sign the release forms

Processing Steps
- Process the materials in preparation for turning over to the repository
- Deliver oral history materials to the repository

ORAL HISTORY TERMS

Oral historians use a variety of terms. While most of these are common, sometimes their meanings are specific to the work of oral historians. As we have seen in Chapter One, this extends to the term *oral history* itself, which can have a variety of meanings.

Listed below are the most common oral history terms and their meanings. These are the terms and definitions used throughout the manual.

Abstract: see recording abstract

Acid-free: There are no consistent standards for acid-free paper. Many consumer products, while labeled acid-free, will develop damaging acids as time goes on. For paper products, acid-free means lignin-free and alkaline, with a pH greater than 7. Lignin is an acidic element found in wood products. Alkaline is the opposite of acidic. For archival markers, acid-free refers to the use of acid-free pigment rather than dye as the coloring medium.

Analog: A recording process that imprints sound in a continuous pattern on magnetic tape.

Archive: A place, often part of a repository, that maintains historical records and documents.

Archivist: A person who cares for and manages collections of historical information, such as oral history, in an archive.

Audit check: An interview processing step in which the recorded interview is carefully listened to while reading the transcript to correct transcribing errors.

Biographical Information Form: A part of the interview record-keeping system, this form contains background information about the narrator.

Copyright: The exclusive legal right to print or otherwise reproduce, publish, or sell copies of original materials, such as oral history interviews, and to license their production and sale by others.

Curate: To manage the long-term care of historical documents for maximum access.

Digital: A recording process that stores sound as bits of data the way a computer stores information.

Donor Form: See release form.

Informant: See narrator.

Interviewee: See narrator.

Interviewer: The person responsible for conducting the oral history interview. This person should have both general and interview-specific background, understand and be able to use open-ended questioning techniques, be able to build effective human relationships in the interview setting, and work to the standards of the Oral History Association.

Interview Information Form: The first step in processing the interview, it identifies the narrator and interviewer, documents the date of the interview and its length, and contains a short abstract or summary of the interview contents.

Life interview: An oral history interview that focuses on one person, usually in a series of interviews. This process results in detailed documentation of the person's life experiences. See also project interview.

Log: See recording abstract.

Master file: A noncirculating file that contains all information about an interview and is permanently kept in the repository as part of the oral history collection.

Narrator (also called interviewee or informant): The person being interviewed. This is a person with firsthand knowledge about the subject of the interview and the ability to effectively communicate the information.

Oral history: Primary-source material created in an interview setting with a witness to or a participant in an event or a way of life for the purpose of preserving the information and making it available to others. The term refers both to the process and the interview itself.

Oral History Association: The U.S.-based professional organization for practitioners of oral history. It supports and encourages an understanding of the ethical principles and standards that guide oral historians in their work.

Oral history interview: The recorded question-and-answer session between an interviewer and narrator characterized by well-focused, clearly stated, open-ended, neutral questions aimed at gathering information not available from other sources.

Oral history project: A series of individual oral history interviews with a number of narrators focusing on one subject or event.

Potential Narrator Information Form: The record-keeping form that contains information about potential project narrators. One form is kept for each name.

Preservation master: The interview recording, kept intact to preserve the interview. Preservation masters are kept in permanent and appropriate storage with the master files; user copies are made from them for access and processing.

Primary source: Firsthand information with no interpretation between the document and the researcher. Examples are oral history recordings and transcripts, diaries, correspondence such as letters from family members, family Bibles, or government records. See also secondary source.

Processing: The steps taken to help make oral history interview information accessible to present and future users.

Processor: The person who works with oral history materials, including recordings, to help make the interview information accessible to users. Processors can include those who develop interview abstracts as well as transcribers.

Project interview: An oral history interview that focuses on a specific topic, place, or event. Interviews for the Library of Congress Veterans History Project, for example, focus on one subject or one part of a narrator's life. See also life interview.

Recording abstract: A list of interview subjects noted in the order in which they were discussed. See also transcript.

Recording equipment: The equipment, audio or video, used to record an interview.

Recording media: The physical materials on which recordings are made.

Release form: The document that transfers copyright of an oral history interview to the designated repository and may list restrictions on use of the interview information. It is signed by both the narrator and the interviewer, and any other person whose voice is heard on the recording, as soon as the interview session ends, even if more interviews are planned with the narrator.

Repository: A facility where oral history materials are deposited and permanently kept.

Secondary source: A publication or other document created using various types of historical information, including primary sources. See also primary source.

Transcribe: Convert spoken information verbatim (word for word) into written form.

Transcript: The verbatim printed copy of interview information. See also recording abstract.

CHAPTER 3

Planning and Budget

When thinking about oral history, it is easy to confuse the interview with the oral history process. The interview is the vehicle through which oral history information is collected. Its success is based on the work that precedes it, the interviewer's skills, and the work that follows it. The planning steps lay the groundwork for enhancing interview effectiveness and help identify the steps for documenting interview context—a plus when using this primary-source information. Whether you choose a life history or a topical oral history project, careful planning and organization are keys to success.

Planning can have other results, too. It may open new and otherwise unrealized avenues of inquiry. It may help project leaders identify information that otherwise might have been missed and help determine the importance of including this information as an interview topic. It may lead to the discovery that what seemed like a simple little project to interview a handful of people could become broader in scope with the opportunity to collect previously unrecognized information.

Working through each of the planning steps in the development of an oral history project or a series of life interviews helps solidify the work and clarify its purpose. Doing so increases the probability for strong, focused, and well-thought-out interviews.

Sometimes a project starts with little more than the intuitive sense that a particular person in the community—often an elderly person—is a storehouse of otherwise unrecorded information about an important event or time in the community's past. If that's the case, consider starting with a preliminary planning project to become familiar with the oral history process and interviewing techniques. Following the planning steps outlined below can encourage planners to focus on the goals and resources needed to develop a successful project. Starting small also can help develop themes or topics, identify a pool of possible narrators, and attract funds to support a larger project.

PLANNING STEPS

> Oral history process planning steps define the basic structure for doing the oral history interview.

Identify Key Leaders and Project Personnel
The first step in the oral history planning process is a basic one—finding people to do the work. Oral history projects are labor intensive. They offer opportunities for many people to be involved in various capacities in addition to the people who will be interviewed. When beginning a project, think first about who will lead and guide it to completion. Look for planners or coordinators who can make the time commitment to see the process through to its end. An oral history project resulting in 15 to 20 interviews can take up to two years to complete.

Whether your project is run by paid staff or volunteers, it helps to designate one or, at the most, two people as coordinators or administrators. An effective project coordinator is dependable, forceful, tactful, dedicated, and single-minded in managing the project. Project coordinators direct the project, determining its purpose, focus, budget, interview themes, number of interviews, processing techniques, and the time frame within which the interviews will be completed.

In addition to the project coordinators, oral history projects have other personnel needs. These usually include:

• Interviewers
• Support staff
• Transcribers

Interviewers are the people who do the oral history interviews. Project coordinators also may be interviewers, but it is important not to confuse the work of the two. Interviewers should be able to give at least 20 to 30 hours per interview. This includes research and interview preparation, doing the interview, processing, and turning interview products over to the project director. The more complex the interview topics and themes, the more preparation time interviewers need.

Projects often have support staff. A secretary or typist can be helpful if the project has money to hire someone or can find a volunteer. A person who is familiar with the equipment and can handle training and maintenance also is an asset.

Finding someone to transcribe the interviews can be a hurdle for oral history project coordinators. Although users of oral history materials often want ongoing access to the voices on the recording, verbatim transcripts are the best way to guarantee long-term access to the interview information. Full transcription ensures the information will remain accessible at least in written form. Transcribing can be done by volunteers or, if projects have funds, coordinators may decide to pay transcribers.

Some oral history projects also include researchers to help with background research about project topics. They can aid project coordinators and interviewers with this important task.

With project personnel in place, it's time to move on to the next planning steps.

Name the Project

Give the project a name. This is how it will be known. It helps give the project definition and a clear and consistent identity. If project letterhead or business cards are printed, use the name on these materials.

Write a Mission Statement

A mission statement defines the purpose of the project. It should be only a few sentences long and should answer the question: "What are we trying to accomplish?" It may sound easy to write but often is one of the more difficult assignments.

The statement includes information on key areas of interest and importance. It defines project focus, but is flexible enough in its language to allow for new directions that might evolve as the project progresses. It can become the yardstick to help project leaders decide who will and will not be interviewed if the number of potential narrators outstrips resources. And it reaffirms the importance of conducting the work to the standards of the Oral History Association.

Several examples of mission statements illustrate these points. The mission statement from the Archives and Special Collections Oral History Program at Purdue University in Indiana states:

> The purpose of the Oral History Program is to record the memories of individuals who have been associated with the University and been direct observers of and participants in its history and evolution. Conducting interviews with key individuals will enrich the University's understanding of its own past while also contributing to the historic record, ensuring that Purdue's legacy is documented, preserved, and made accessible to researchers and the general public.[1]

The University of California, San Francisco (UCSF) Oral History Program mission statement identifies its focus on biomedical research and medical education:

> The central mission of our program is to explore, analyze, and preserve the historical record of this institution, and thereby significantly enhance documentation of the history of American biomedical research and medical education in the twentieth century.[2]

The Youngstown (Ohio) State University Oral History Program describes its focus and states that it works to the standards of the Oral History Association:

Oral History Program—Mission Statement

- To develop and conduct oral history projects important to the historical record of the people of the state of Ohio.
- To provide a diverse, coherent, and integrated body of sources for use by scholars, students, and the interested public.
- To conduct its collecting and processing activities in accordance with the highest standards of the Oral History Association.
- To play a role in regional and national professional oral history organizations.
- To assist community groups and organizations within the state with the collection of oral histories through training workshops and lectures.
- To play an active role in the instructional programs of the university, especially in training graduate and undergraduate students in the field of oral history collection and research.[3]

Choose a Repository

If a project already is operating under the sponsorship of a historical society, library, or museum, choosing a repository is not an issue. But if that is not the case, finding a permanent home for project materials is an important decision. It will determine who will have ongoing curatorial responsibility for care of all project products, including permanent storage of and access to media, interview information, transcripts, and all related materials. It is a responsibility not to be taken lightly. Suitable candidates for a permanent repository will depend on available facilities and staff.

Project leaders should approach a repository and discuss possible ownership of oral history materials as early as possible in the planning process. Repositories often have requirements for accepting collections. Leaders will want to make sure the interview materials will be held by a repository that has the ability to safeguard the collection and make it as widely available as possible.

Look for a repository that will manage all project materials in accordance with the prevailing archival and curatorial standards and the standards of the Oral History Association. Review written policies governing access to and care of collections. Look for a rights and permissions statement clarifying use and copyright guidelines. Discuss the possibility of depositing copies of interview materials in other accessible locations. And remember that the Internet is not a repository. Use it to disseminate project information, but never consider it a permanent repository.

If, for some reason, oral history project materials are not put in a standard repository, the chances of their being lost increase exponentially. Oral history projects that end up permanently stashed under someone's bed or in a closet or attic are as inaccessible to the general public as items lost from the Internet.

See Chapter Eight for a more detailed discussion of repository selection and the ongoing care and access guidelines for oral history materials.

Prepare to Be Offered Additional Materials

When completed, an oral history collection can include media, server space, transcripts or interview logs, and narrator files—and that may not be all. Often, as a result of an interview, a narrator will offer the project historic photographs (which may either be copied and returned or kept), other archival materials, and artifacts. When accepted, these materials become part of the project collection and need to be cared for at the designated repository. Appendix A provides sample forms for handling these materials as part of the interview.

Select a Project Advisory Board

The project advisory board is a group of people who can provide support for the project. Do not confuse this group with the leaders or coordinators. The advisory board's purpose is to help find funding sources and additional support options, help with project needs such as legal advice when called upon to do so, and help identify potential narrators. It is a way of building a network of project support.

The people on the advisory board are not responsible for intensive planning work. All, however, should be committed to the project and its goals and should thoroughly understand the role of advisory board members and why they have been asked to serve. They may be community leaders who will help find funding sources or equipment when needed, experts on the general subject of the interviews, or those with a good grounding in history chosen to help guide the project on the most effective use of its time and resources. A liaison with a sponsoring institution also often serves on this board. Choose advisory board members for the support they can give to the project or their access to the types of expertise the project needs.

An advisory board does not have to meet regularly. Often a meeting at the beginning of the project is sufficient with periodic follow-up reports to let board members know how the project is progressing. Some boards also meet when the project is completed to help celebrate the results. During the project individual advisory board members may be asked to answer questions or to help with a particular phase. Even if an advisory board does not meet regularly, keep board members informed with periodic progress reports.

Establish a Project Timeframe

A project timeframe establishes goals for project milestones—completing the research, preparing interview outlines, completing interviews. Allot time for:

- identifying interviewers and providing interviewer training
- selecting narrators
- research, including narrator-specific work
- scheduling and conducting interviews
- processing interviews.

Define blocks of time for various project tasks. The time it takes to adequately prepare for the interviews, acquire good equipment, do the interviews, and process them effectively can take a toll on even the most enthusiastic project participants. Developing a timeframe helps you think through the project, identifying the necessary tasks and the time that can realistically be allotted to complete each one. Remember that oral history projects can change as new information is uncovered, so be prepared to remain flexible rather than slavishly adhering to your timeframe. But laying out expectations, even if they change during the project, can help everyone better understand its needs.

*Create a Record-Keeping System
and Establish Procedures*

After reaching agreement with a project repository, begin to develop record-keeping systems. A relatively invisible part of project development, record-keeping provides continuity and support necessary for both interviewer and narrator. Don't get bogged down in paperwork, but developing standard forms at the outset can help keep a project on track. See sample forms in Appendix A.

Some of the most commonly used forms are listed and described here. They include:

- donor (legal release) form
- biographical information form
- oral history interview information form
- potential narrator form
- master log form
- artifact and archival inventory forms

The donor or legal release form provides for transfer of copyright to the repository that will hold the interview materials. Transfer of copyright allows future researchers to have access to the interview information. It is an essential part of the support materials for an interview and must be signed if the interview is to become part of the available primary-source materials in the repository's collections. Failure to do so leaves ownership of the interview with those whose voices are on the recording. Fill out the form and sign it after each interview, even if another interview is planned with the same narrator. For more information, see Chapter Four.

The biographical information form contains basic biographical information about a narrator. Depending on how the project is organized, it may be filled out at the beginning of the interview or during a preliminary meeting or telephone conversation between the interviewer and narrator. It documents who the narrator is, both for project purposes and for the benefit of future researchers.

The interviewer should fill in the oral history information form as soon as possible after an interview. It lists the names of the narrator and interviewer, the project name, interview date and length, and identifies number and type of media. It also confirms that the donor form has been signed, and it contains a one- to three-paragraph statement about the interview contents. This form provides immediate access to the interview information before full processing has been completed.

The potential narrator information form is an important element of your record-keeping system because it helps you keep track of possible narrators. Project research often will uncover the names of people whose information could be important to the project, and additional names can surface as news about your project spreads. The potential narrator information form is a place to keep up-to-date information about all such prospective narrators, including full names, home and work addresses, telephone and fax numbers, e-mail addresses, and other contact information. It also should include a brief summary about the person's background and information he or she can contribute to the project.

> The donor form transfers copyright to the designated owner. Always remember the narrator and the interviewer should sign a donor form after each interview.

Other suggested forms are the master log form and archival, artifact, and manuscript inventory forms. The master log form identifies all contacts with narrators. It shows the progress of each interview, its length, and processing status, and provides a capsule summary of project progress at any point in time.

The archival, artifact, and manuscript inventory forms list additional materials the narrator might offer an interviewer during the interview. Oral history interviews are generally done in a narrator's home or other community location, and interviewers often learn about additional information, including photographs, memorabilia, and other materials that narrators sometimes wish to give to the project repository. The inventory forms help keep track of these materials, identifying items and their donors.

Some projects use a Letter of Agreement for Volunteer Interviewers and a Letter of Agreement for Transcribers. Each spells out the responsibilities of the position and has a place for a signature. Projects using paid interviewers will want to become familiar with

PROJECT MASTER LOG

Narrator	Interviewer	Interview Date	Release Signed (note type)	Draft Transcript to Narrator	Processing Done (note type and by whom)	Artifacts/ Photos (cross reference to form)	Put in Repository
Jane Doe	Mary Smith	9/10/08	9/10/08	11/2/08	3/20/09 Transcript by AR	Yes— see form	4/1/09
James Doe	Mary Smith	11/20/08	11/20/08 Restricted	12/15/08		NA	
John Doe	Mary Smith	1/25/09	1/25/09	2/20/09	3/19/09 Tape/log by MR	NA	4/1/09
Julie Doe	Mary Smith	2/10/09	2/10/09			Yes— see form	

Figure 3.1.   An example of a filled-out Master Log Form.

the Work-Made-for-Hire Doctrine and the Work-Made-for-Hire Agreement. For more information, see *Oral History and the Law*.[4]

Finally, a noncirculating master file is a place to keep information about each narrator and interview. It usually contains:

- background and contact information of the narrator
- correspondence with the narrator
- notes from conversations with the narrator, whether by telephone or in person
- biographical information form
- potential narrator information form
- completed interview information form
- original copy of the signed donor form
- interview outline (topics and questions)
- narrator-specific research materials
- interview notes
- lists of people and place names mentioned during the interview with the narrator's spelling corrections
- a photograph of the narrator, often taken in the interview setting
- a more formal photo given by the narrator, if desired
- a draft of the transcript containing the narrator's comments and corrections

Determine the Equipment to Use in the Interviews and in Transcribing

Recording equipment decisions often provoke lively discussions. This also is one of the larger oral history expenses. Equipment decisions include whether to use audio or video, how to combine the two if both are to be used, and what types of equipment will produce final products that fit the budget and serve the project's needs. For more information about oral history equipment, see Chapter Five.

Develop a Publicity Plan

Be sure to give some thought to creating a project publicity plan. This is an essential, but often overlooked, element of any successful oral history project. The oral history interviews, when completed, will represent an important addition of new information or new perspectives to the historical record. Publicizing the collection's existence should not be neglected. Project publicity includes everything from letting people know it is taking place to encouraging use of the completed interviews. Publicity will help all steps of the

project by encouraging support—financial and material—and maintaining participant and community enthusiasm.

A publicity plan can include a brochure that describes the project and lists the names of coordinators and supporters. This can be useful both for the general public and as a handout for prospective narrators. Project coordinators also may want to print project stationery as a way of reinforcing the project's public identity.

Sometimes project coordinators think it will help generate good publicity if they issue a press release asking for would-be narrators to step forward. Resist the temptation to do that unless you've found absolutely no other way to identify potential narrators. A public request for narrators implies a promise to interview anyone who comes forth, which may not be in the best interests of your project. The choice of narrators is better made through careful research.

Although some work on the publicity plan will take place at the beginning of the project, most will occur after the information has been collected and the project is complete. At that time, announce project results to the general public. Send brief press releases to all local news media and other organizations—local, state, national, or international—that might have an interest in the information you've collected.

Train Your Interviewers

The ideal situation is to find trained oral history interviewers who are familiar with a project's subject. But whether you are using experienced or novice interviewers, arrange for interviewer training and project orientation sessions as part of the planning and development process. This is essential to creating good oral history interviews. An orientation and training workshop should include discussion of your project's goals as well as general background about the oral history process. Would-be interviewers, no matter how much experience they have, need to learn about the unique characteristics of each project. And as new interviewers join a project, follow-up training always should be offered.

Training interviewers is integral to a project's success. Haphazard or insufficient training is certain to be a project's downfall. Even the best-planned oral history projects can fizzle if interviewers lack the skills they need to get started or to improve their work once the interviewing phase is under way.

Training is available from a variety of sources. The Oral History Association's annual fall meetings always include informative workshops for beginning and advanced oral history practitioners, and state or regional oral history organizations often schedule workshops as well. State historical societies, state or regional museum associations, local colleges and universities, and state humanities councils can be resources for oral history training. And experienced oral historians often are available to create workshops customized to meet a project's needs.

This covers the overview of the oral history planning steps. The next step is to develop a project budget.

DEVELOP A PROJECT BUDGET

Oral history is an exciting and invigorating process. But the reality of financial needs can stop a good project before it gets off the ground. It helps to create a budget early in the planning process and to include all possible project costs. With this, you can begin to determine realistically what you can and cannot accomplish. Even if your project will be staffed largely by volunteers, it will incur expenses. While some of those may be met through volunteered time or donated materials, it is still important at the outset to determine realistically what funds will be required and when. The costs of developing and carrying out an oral history project often are underestimated. Mapping out expected costs early in the project helps everyone understand its needs.

> Developing a project budget helps determine costs. A budget is helpful even if a project is volunteer-run.

What are the financial needs of an oral history project? Oral historians ask this question almost as often as they ask what equipment to use. Oral history is not cheap. Committed volunteers can help underwrite project costs and provide considerable manpower. But unless everything—time, space, and materials—is donated, projects need cash to survive.

Oral history is labor intensive. If you think only in terms of interview costs, the project will be woefully underfunded. Although its most visible product, the interview, may take just a few hours, careful preparation beforehand and meticulous processing afterward are time-consuming. Adequate budgeting for that time plus the cost of equipment and other supplies is a critical part of successfully completing an oral history project. Identifying all project costs and sources of revenue can make the difference between a good idea and a successfully completed project.

The full costs of an oral history project are not immediately obvious, as many project organizers have found to their dismay. Include the following elements in a project budget:

One-Time or Non-Recurring Expenses:
- recording equipment, including carrying cases
- microphones and accessories, including cables
- duplicating equipment
- transcribing equipment
- consultant fee, if needed

Overhead Costs:
- administration, including salaries for any paid project staff
- advisory board meetings when necessary, including per diems for advisory board members
- honoraria and per diems for project guest speakers and others as needed
- interviewer training
- photocopying
- postage
- telephone, fax
- printing costs, such as letterhead, business cards, project brochures
- office space
- office equipment, such as file cabinets
- other costs, including equipment repair and unexpected items

Interview Costs:
- interview research and preparation
- media for each interview and for all copies that will need to be made
- payment to interviewers (as needed)
- payment to videographer, if used
- payment to transcriber, if used
- interview processing (audio, video)
- travel (interview research/interview)

Budget Discussion

Each of the budget elements is a project cost, whether donated, in-kind, or purchased. Among all project costs, equipment is one of the largest. Once purchased, it will be available for the duration of the project. The number of recorders and microphones needed will be based on available funds, the size of the project, and the number of project interviewers.

The amount and type of media will depend on the number of narrators you'll be interviewing. Digital recordings are made on one type of media and saved on another. Plan to save an interview in at least two forms and to make at least three additional copies of each recording: a processing copy, a public user copy, and a courtesy copy for the narrator.

Photocopying, printing, and postage are standard project costs and will depend on the size and scope of the project. Travel costs should cover both research and interview needs.

Processing costs support making copies of the interviews as well as abstracting, indexing, and transcribing. Transcribing is the ideal—but more expensive—option. It involves taking the time to type out interview information word-for-word and then checking the written material for accuracy. Abstract and interview logs are generally reimbursed by the hour, while transcribers are paid either by the page or by the interview hour—a set fee for each hour of interview regardless of how long the transcribing takes.

Transcribing costs vary widely depending on location and transcriber experience. Medical transcribers and court transcribers are an option. If your project uses transcribers with this background, make sure they are adept at the specifics of transcribing oral history interviews. Experienced, professional oral history transcribers advertise in professional publications and also can be located through inquiries to institutions that sponsor oral history projects.

Personnel costs vary, depending on project participants. Is this a volunteer-run project, a project run by paid staff, or a combination of the two? An estimate of personnel costs can be determined by looking at salaries of equivalent staff at local museums and libraries. Interviewers sometimes are paid by the interview. Videographers are paid by the hour, studio hour, or interview. Generally narrators are not paid, although in some circumstances, a gift may be given.

Oral history projects often rely on volunteers. Doing oral history requires firm resolve and many hours of time on the part of project participants. Volunteers should make every effort to keep to the schedules and guidelines the coordinators establish. Projects in which this understanding has been well defined from the beginning have the best chance of success.

Whether using volunteer or paid staff, oral history training is an essential expense. A workshop for project participants, including planners, interviewers, and processors, can save everyone unnecessary mistakes and loss of time. Attending a one-day workshop to learn and practice appropriate interviewing techniques

should be a minimum expectation for volunteers who want to be involved in a project. Don't forget to budget for workshop training costs.

Finally, to help determine the number of interviews a project can reasonably afford, develop a per-interview cost. Identify all costs associated with an interview, using an average interview length of two hours. This will provide a realistic rule of thumb for per-interview costs. Multiply per-interview costs by the number of planned project interviews for a ballpark total interview cost estimate.

Find Financial Support and Funding Sources

Finding funding can be an ongoing process. Oral history projects take time and can be expensive. Unless full funding already exists, start laying the groundwork for obtaining funding as soon as you have defined the project and developed a budget. Even volunteer projects have costs that donated time and materials cannot cover. Funding sources can include outright grants, loans of equipment and other materials, in-kind contributions, self-funding by institutions, grants from state or local historical societies or state humanities councils, and programs run through public libraries. Experienced oral historians know that while all are good options, the available amount of per-project funds from each of these sources often is relatively small and that many or all may be necessary to successfully complete a project.

Competition is keen for grants from national sources. The National Endowment for the Humanities, for example, funds oral history work, although such projects have to show evidence of national significance, pass rigorous reviews, and show strong evidence of planning and preparation. Many projects look for funds from other sources to support initial planning work before considering an application for federal funds.

Educational institutions often develop and carry out oral history projects, as do libraries, archives, and museums. Several major colleges and universities have ongoing flagship programs with work done primarily by faculty and research assistants. Oral history projects at colleges and universities developed with volunteer support and run through the college archives also are becoming increasingly common. Community members interested in documenting specific events or time periods may want to explore college or university programs to discuss possible collaborative efforts.

Local secondary school history or social studies teachers are another possible source of support. Although class schedules and days are full for students and teachers, the possibility of school-community collaboration may be of interest. Teachers across the country have successfully integrated oral history into the curriculum, offering students an exciting opportunity for hands-on learning while preserving community history that might otherwise be lost.

Professional associations, businesses, and interest groups related to a project's theme are potential sources of financial support. Some may be willing to provide in-kind (non-cash, donated) support such as offering a place to meet or providing supplies. Local governments and corporations may be other sources.

City- and state-based foundations and local businesses can be sources of funds if project purposes meet their grant guidelines. Local libraries often have a sec-

tion on grants opportunities that can be a help. Many nonprofit organizations and local foundations sponsor grant-writing workshops that can help in locating funding sources and writing grant proposals. Some coordinators find private sources, but if these sources are used, take care to ensure donors do not control project results.

Chapter Five provides detailed information about the types of equipment and media recommended for oral history projects. The standards are high because using good equipment maximizes the life of the interview. But don't be deterred by the price tag and think that you must abandon the project if you cannot immediately go out and purchase such equipment. This is another area where community sources of support may be able to help. Organizations that may not be able or willing to fund interviews might fund equipment purchases. Other agencies, including radio and television stations, school districts, or state historical societies, might be willing to loan equipment to the project or permit you to use specialized equipment such as that needed to duplicate interviews. Borrowing equipment, in fact, is sometimes preferable to buying it.

Finding funding sources does not mean just looking for outright grants, but identifying any and all possible means of support. Local businesses might provide in-kind support for equipment, media, printing, postage, or photocopying. Community-based organizations may be willing to help with travel expenses and transcribing interviews. All can help assure successful completion of a project.

Project coordinators should keep careful record of gifts and loans of materials and time because in-kind support can help show potential funders the value of commitment to the project. Start keeping track of all time and materials beginning with the first planning meetings and continue this practice throughout the life of the project. And, as a reminder, keep in mind the purpose of the project you want to develop: even while gratefully accepting help and support, don't let the wishes of supporters influence project outcomes. This is not easy, but is important to the final results.

This discussion of budgeting for an oral history project does not include the costs of creating products from oral history interviews, such as websites, museum exhibits, books, pamphlets, or CDs. It focuses only on the development of the oral history interview as a primary-source document. If you wish to develop additional products after the project has been completed, you will want to budget for this, too.

Support for oral history projects varies depending on the community, project coordinators, and available resources. As with all stages of project development, however, good planning will help. Always let potential supporters know what you want to accomplish and why it is important. Show them a clear plan of work and a realistic, clearly defined budget. Explain what the results of the project will be and how the oral history materials will be made available in the future. Finding funding is one of the most time-consuming parts of project coordination, but it can be one of the most rewarding.

NOTES

1. Purdue University, Archives and Special Collections Oral History Program, http://www.lib.purdue.edu/spcol/ oralhistory/, accessed September 8, 2008.

2. University of California School of Medicine, UCSF Oral History Program, http://www.dahsm.medschool.ucsf .edu/oralHistory/, accessed September 8, 2008.

3. Youngstown State University Oral History Program, http://www.as.ysu.edu/~histpres/orhistms.htm, accessed September 8, 2008.

4. John A. Neuenschwander, *Oral History and the Law*, 3rd ed. (Carlisle, PA: Oral History Association, 2002): 32–33 and Appendix C.

CHAPTER 4

Legal and Ethical Considerations

What legal and ethical considerations apply to the practice of oral history? Oral history projects often are born of a desire to capture the memories of elderly community members or to increase knowledge about places or historic events. But enthusiastic planners often have no idea they're embarking on a project with important legal and ethical dimensions. This chapter will:

- introduce the basic legal and ethical considerations that underpin oral history practice;
- discuss how legal and ethical issues affect project planning and administration, equipment decisions, processing, and the end use of the oral history interview;
- discuss the legal and ethical dimensions of rapidly changing technology and financial issues that affect oral history practice;
- outline special considerations stemming from federal regulations that affect oral history work on many college and university campuses.

But this chapter will not:

- offer a shortcut to law school;
- provide legal advice;
- recommend archives management policies. Many legal and ethical considerations affect procedures for handling interview recordings and transcripts. This chapter will describe the range of issues and options to consider, but it is no substitute for professional archival information, which can be obtained from qualified archivists. The Society of American Archivists and the American Association for State and Local History are good sources of information about archives management issues.

The primary legal framework for oral history work rests on the established legal premise that an oral history interview creates a copyrightable document as soon as the recorder is turned off at the end of an interview session. Decide during the planning process how to secure copyright (the exclusive legal right to reproduce, distribute, display, perform, or create derivative works) from the interview's creators and how to handle responsibly the materials your project creates. This chapter will help you accomplish that.

Oral histories came to be treated as copyrightable documents in the earliest days of institutional oral history practice at Columbia University where the interviews or oral memoirs were deemed analogous to written autobiographies, which authors clearly could copyright. Over time, the practice evolved of asking narrators to give their copyright interest to institutions sponsoring oral history programs, thus alleviating the need for the narrators themselves to control access to the materials. Narrators or interviewers legally could insist on retaining their copyright interest and simply grant project sponsors permission to use their interviews in a specific way—with or without certain restrictions. Such arrangements, however, are cumbersome at best.

Instead, institutions that sponsor oral history programs or repositories that include oral histories in their collections typically hold the copyright for those materials and are responsible for making them accessible under whatever conditions they deem appropriate, subject to any restrictions noted on the donor forms. Transfer of copyright is consistent with the legal and ethical standards promulgated by the Oral History Association (OHA), the national professional organization of oral history practitioners. Moreover, most institutions or organizations that sponsor or maintain oral history collections would be reluctant to accept interviews without clear legal rights to use them and make them accessible to others, which a copyright transfer insures. While rare situations might occur, such as a highly prominent narrator who insisted on having an intellectual property lawyer negotiate a unique donor form, the vast majority of oral history interviews do not fall into that category. Customized donor forms for each interview in a collection would be an archivist's nightmare, and management issues associated with such one-of-a-kind legal documents should be considered carefully in a project's planning stages.

Indeed, a host of legal and ethical issues arises at virtually every stage of creating an oral history. The OHA describes in its publication *Evaluation Guidelines: Principles and Standards of the Oral History Association* the ethical principles and standards that guide oral historians. (The complete text of that publication is included in Appendix B.) These principles and standards outline an oral historian's responsibilities to narrators, to the public, and to the profession and the responsibilities of institutions that sponsor oral history programs or serve as repositories for collections of oral history materials.

The ethical framework that the OHA describes is based on these premises:

- Narrators invited to be interviewed for a project should fairly reflect all sides of the topic or issue being pursued.
- A narrator is entitled to respect for his or her story, even if it differs markedly from customary interpretations of an event.
- A narrator must give fully informed consent to participate in an oral history interview. Full information includes a thorough description of the purposes of the project as well as the expected disposition and dissemination of the materials.
- An interviewer should be well trained, for only a competent interviewer who has prepared thoroughly will be able to conduct an interview that goes beyond superficial treatment of the topic and results in the collection of new information of lasting value.
- An interviewer should document fully the preparation, methods, and circumstances of an interview, for only with such background information can future users of the interview make informed judgments about its content.
- Rewards and recognition that come to an oral history project should be shared with narrators and their communities.
- Whoever owns the final product, whether an individual or an institution, should maintain the highest professional standards in preserving the oral history interviews and making them available to others.

If you're planning an oral history project, become thoroughly familiar with the OHA *Evaluation Guidelines* before starting. You also should study *Oral History and the Law*, by John A. Neuenschwander,[1] a past OHA president, history professor, lawyer, and municipal judge. Originally published as part of the OHA pamphlet series, *Oral History and the Law* is the single most complete source of information about this topic. Now published in book form by Oxford University Press, it provides considerably more detail about legal issues potentially affecting oral historians than this manual can offer, and it should be a part of every oral historian's library. But even it is not a substitute for competent legal advice, which all projects should seek during the planning stages as a way to prevent legal problems down the road. Project coordinators should provide their institution's legal staff with copies of the *Oral History and the Law*, too.

The rest of this chapter outlines the legal and ethical issues you should consider at each step of an oral history project.

PLANNING A PROJECT

The first—and most important—legal issue project coordinators must address is who will own the materials the project ultimately creates. While it may seem premature to think about what should be done with materials that don't yet exist, it is fundamental to the rest of the planning process because it determines who will hold the copyright to the oral history interviews, maintain the materials, and govern access to them.

> The donor or legal release form transfers copyright to the designated owner. Always remember that the narrator and the interviewer should sign a donor form after each interview.

Because an oral history interview is a copyrightable document from the moment the interview ends, both interviewer and narrator—and anyone else whose voice is on the recording—have a copyright interest in the material on the recording. No one else may use it without their permission. Thus, to make the oral history interviews readily available for researchers and others to use, both interviewer and narrator should sign a donor or legal release form at the end of each interview session giving their copyright interest to the project.

PROJECT ADMINISTRATION

Handling the paperwork an oral history project generates is an ongoing responsibility of project coordinators. Perhaps the single most important piece of paper associated with oral history projects is the donor form or legal release form, which gives the project repository (the place that owns and maintains the materials) the right to use and disseminate the oral history materials. Unless the project has a signed release form that properly transfers copyright for each oral history interview, public access to the information is possible only if the narrators and interviewers or their heirs grant permission to specific requests for access, a prospect most repositories would deem impractical and unworkable. Equally impractical from a repository's standpoint would be donor forms in which the narrator retained copyright and authorized the repository to use the material only in certain ways.

If you're working with a repository that already has an oral history collection, the repository itself likely will dictate the nature of the donor form required. If, however, the oral history materials will be held by an institution unfamiliar with such release forms, you'll need to write one, with the advice of informed legal counsel. It is worth noting that oral history might be an unfamiliar concept to many lawyers. You'll need to be prepared to explain thoroughly what you are doing and provide relevant materials, such as Neuenschwander's book. Above all, be prepared to insist that any documents narrators and interviewers are asked to sign be written in commonly understood language, not legalistic mumbo jumbo. Narrators cannot give informed consent if they cannot understand the document they're asked to sign. Simple, one-page forms are the best. Sample release forms can be found in Appendix A. Other samples are included in *Oral History and the Law*. These can be a useful guide, but resist the temptation merely to copy these release forms or forms from another oral history project. Instead, be sure the donor agreement you use meets YOUR project's needs.

A donor form can be either a contract or a deed of gift. To be complete legally and thus enforceable, each of these documents must contain specific elements that are discussed briefly below. The key distinction between the two is that a contract must provide for what is known legally as "consideration," or payment. Some oral history projects use a contract form, stipulating, for example, a token $1.00 payment or promising the narrator a bound copy of the interview transcript. Considerably more common is the deed of gift form, a voluntary transfer of property without any payment. Indeed some projects call their donor form a "gift of personal memoir." Be sure you don't create a hybrid donor form that includes elements of both a contract and a deed of gift. Such hybrids are more difficult to defend legally because they fall outside the boundaries of the conventional legal framework.

Whatever form you use, it should include:

- clear identification of the name of the narrator;
- clear identification of the project repository;
- a statement that the narrator is transferring "legal title and all literary property rights to the interview, including copyright" to the repository;
- a place for the narrator to sign;
- a place for the interviewer to sign.

Federal copyright law specifies that for a copyright transfer to be valid, it must be in writing and signed by the copyright owner. So be sure the donor form contains a specific reference to copyright, and not some generic, legal-sounding language about "all rights, title, and interest."

Donor forms also may include restrictions on how interviews may or may not be used. Such restrictions might allow use of the material in various formats for nonprofit use but prohibit use of the materials for commercial purposes without the narrator's written consent or that of his or her heirs. Try to resist the temptation to create overly specific lists of possible future uses of the material, which run the risk of creating an inflexible project that legally cannot be used in new creative formats.

Of particular interest in recent years is the proliferation of oral history projects that choose to put materials on the Internet. The ethical arguments over the merits of Internet dissemination of oral history materials will be discussed below, but any project that contemplates doing so should include in its donor form a specific reference to electronic distribution as well as archival deposit and copyright.

Holding the copyright to the oral history materials might clearly give a project the legal right to put materials online, but most oral historians would consider it a serious breach of ethics to do so unless narrators are fully informed about the intent to do so and agree to it in advance. Many oral history collections now considering Internet dissemination of materials face the daunting prospect of retroactively seeking permission from narrators (or their heirs) whose memories were recorded long before the digital age. So even if project coordinators don't currently plan electronic distribution of oral history materials, they should consider including a specific reference allowing it to alleviate future complications. Narrators always may stipulate that they do not wish such distribution of an interview, which should be noted clearly in the signed legal agreement.

Other unusual situations occasionally occur that will affect the donor form. As you plan your project, consider possibilities such as those discussed below and decide how to handle them should they arise.

- Narrators—or interviewers—who are reluctant to assign copyright to the project because they want to use the material for their own written memoirs or other work before the interviews are opened to the general public. You can handle this dilemma by including a sentence in your donor forms stipulating that the narrator or interviewer has the right to first use of the material for a specified period of time. This amounts to the copyright holder—the project's sponsor—granting a license for use of the material. Alternatively, language could be included stipulating that the gift of copyright doesn't preclude use of the interview itself by the narrator or interviewer. These kinds of situations call for careful consultation with the project's legal adviser to arrive at language that meets everyone's needs.

- Narrators who want to close access to all or part of their interviews. This usually occurs when a narrator has something unflattering, highly controversial, or potentially defamatory to say about someone. Such information can be important to the interview because of the context it provides, and, in these unusual circumstances, an oral history project may agree to close access to the interview materials for a specified number of years. Defamation issues will be discussed more fully below in connection with processing and archiving oral history materials. But you should understand—and should make sure narrators understand—that while materials can be closed to researchers, they are unlikely to be protected from subpoena. As Neuenschwander has repeatedly noted, U.S. courts generally have not recognized an archival privilege or scholar's privi-

lege analogous to the legal protections that apply to communications between husbands and wives or doctors and patients. Similarly, state and federal open records laws can affect the ability of a project sponsored by a government agency to restrict access to oral history materials. Open records laws vary, so you'll need to determine what conditions prevail in your jurisdiction. A sample of donor form language allowing a restriction may be found in Appendix A.

- Narrators who wish to remain anonymous. Oral history projects occasionally seek interviews with AIDS patients, battered women, drug addicts, or members of political, religious, or other groups who fear persecution for sharing their life stories. If your project entertains the notion of interviewing vulnerable people and protecting their identities, it is imperative that you seek legal advice on how or whether that can be accomplished.

- Volunteer or freelance interviewers who refuse to relinquish work in progress if the oral history project disintegrates. Actually, if that happens, it's likely too late to prevent messy entanglements. That's why you should have volunteer or freelance interviewers—or anyone working for the project as an independent contractor—sign an agreement at the outset making clear who has rights to the ownership and possession of the oral history materials in case the project ends before it's completed. Again, Neuenschwander offers a complete discussion of this issue.

ORAL HISTORY INTERVIEWING EQUIPMENT

While equipment selection is not a legal matter, myriad other considerations affect the choice of equipment for an oral history project. Chapter Five provides complete details on the technological aspects of the many audio and video equipment choices available. But equipment choice and use also has an ethical dimension you should keep in mind. Here are some examples:

- While all recording equipment has a presence in the interview setting, video equipment in particular can be more intrusive than the equipment needed for an audio-only interview. Oral historians need to be sensitive to narrators' reluctance to appear on camera and respect their right to refuse to participate in a video interview.

- Oral history projects that choose to record interviews on video should make sure camera operators avoid unflattering camera angles and lighting that create harsh portrayals of narrators. While a video oral history interview is not a documentary or a polished, rehearsed performance, it should not portray people negatively.

- Some oral historians argue that there is an ethical dimension to selecting recording equipment that fails to meet the test of time. As this manual makes clear, good oral history requires substantial planning and thorough research. To do that, and then have the interview materials themselves deteriorate rapidly or otherwise become unusable, is a disservice to everyone who participates in a project, but particularly to narrators whose time, energy, and memories made the project possible. Make every effort to maximize the quality of the equipment you choose, within the limits of your financial resources.

- Whatever the equipment choices, interviewers always should be thoroughly trained in its use. Failure to do so disrespects narrators by wasting their time and resulting in a low-quality interview of limited usefulness.

- Video interviews have greater potential for attracting interest from video production companies and other commercial interests, and narrators should be told that in the interest of fully informing them about the nature of the project. Some repositories, however, do not allow commercial use of their materials.

PROJECT BUDGET

As Chapter Three describes, well-done oral history projects don't come cheap, but creative project coordinators become adept at finding resources. Projects sponsored by companies and large institutions often are self-funded, and those sponsored by local nonprofit, volunteer-run organizations often rely on funds from a wide variety of sources.

No matter what your sources of funds, always strive to maintain the intellectual integrity of the project and guard against any attempt by financial backers to control the content of the project or dictate topics or themes that must be pursued as a condition of funding. Publicity about the project, public exhibits, or other materials developed as a result of the project and permanent records of the collection should include information about sources of funds or project sponsors.

INTERVIEW PREPARATION

The preparation required before an oral history interview is fundamental to its success, and, like the other steps in the oral history process, it has an ethical dimension.

Oral historians must conduct background research to the highest standards of scholarly integrity, taking care to document fully the sources of information consulted in the project's research phase. Providing such documentation makes it possible for future users of an oral history collection to put the interviews in context and understand the background against which the interviews took place.

The preparation phase, discussed in detail in Chapter Six, is the point at which potential narrators are identified, and here, again, ethical issues arise. Narrators invited to participate in an oral history project should reflect the full range of perspectives about the topic or issue on which the oral history project focuses. This sometimes can be difficult precisely because oral history projects aim to find and collect previously undocumented accounts of often controversial events. But oral historians with a strong sense of ethics will commit themselves to creating as complete a historical contribution as possible.

THE INTERVIEW SETTING

As Chapter Six also advises, practical considerations govern most of the decisions about where interviews take place. But just as equipment choices have an ethical dimension, so also do the choices about interview setting. While an oral history interview is not a relaxed social occasion, you can maximize the quality of an interview by assuring that it takes place where the narrator will be most comfortable. This is particularly important when narrators are elderly or have special physical needs. Likewise, arrangements for the interview should not be unduly intrusive or disruptive, nor should they in any way exploit a narrator. Ethical oral historians, particularly in a video oral history project, never should try to coax narrators to conduct their interviews in settings that would make them uncomfortable, no matter how visually interesting the settings might be.

THE INTERVIEW

Ethical conduct of the oral history interview is fundamental to the integrity of an oral history project.

While Chapter Seven describes the process in detail, any discussion of oral history legal and ethical issues must stress the importance of respect for narrators and their stories as the underpinning of ethical interviewing. Interviewers show that respect by:

- adequate preparation and training that enables them to ask probing questions in a professional manner;
- familiarity with the equipment so they can operate it with confidence, thus assuring proper recording and preventing the equipment from becoming the focus of the interview;
- being sensitive to the diversity of their narrators and their perspectives and shunning thoughtless stereotypes that cloud understanding of people and issues;
- refraining from making promises that can't be fulfilled, such as guaranteeing that the oral history interview will be used or published;
- assuring that the narrator and interviewer properly sign the donor forms at the conclusion of each interview session. Some oral historians advocate summarizing the content of the form while the recorder is turned on—either at the beginning or end of the interview—and getting the narrator's verbal agreement with the terms of the document in addition to the concurrence in writing.

PROCESSING THE INTERVIEW

Processing and archival issues that relate to how the content of an oral history interview is to be made public raise a host of legal and ethical concerns.

If you plan for full transcriptions of the interviews, narrators customarily are permitted to review drafts of the transcripts to make corrections before the materials are made public. To streamline that process but still maintain the ethical duty to allow narrators to review their transcripts, some oral history projects include in their release form a clause saying that the narrator has the right to review the transcript before it is put in final form. The document transfers copyright to the project, but commits the project to returning the transcript before making it public. Such release forms also often specify that if the narrator fails to return the transcript within a specified period of time—at least 30 days—it will be assumed that the transcript is correct and thus can become part of the oral history collection.

In addition to the copyright issue discussed earlier, another major legal issue comes into play in process-

ing and archiving oral history materials. Make sure you have a procedure for reviewing the content of interviews to see if they contain potentially defamatory statements, which *Ballentine's Law Dictionary* defines as "anything which is injurious to the good name or reputation of another person, or which tends to bring him into disrepute." Defamatory statements can be spoken (slander) or written (libel).[2]

Neuenschwander's *Oral History and the Law* makes clear that oral history collections that include potentially defamatory statements made by narrators could be found equally guilty of defamation for disseminating such statements as the narrators who made the statements in the first place. While it's unclear just how frequently oral history narrators offer a slanderous remark, you need to be aware of the possibility and need to be sure that interviewers alert project coordinators whenever such statements occur in an interview. Generally, words held to be defamatory relate to accusations of criminal, unethical, or immoral behavior, professional incompetence, financial irresponsibility, or association with despicable people.[3]

> Oral history projects need to be aware of the potential legal pitfalls of disseminating potentially defamatory statements narrators might make. Generally words held to be defamatory relate to accusations of criminal, unethical, or immoral behavior, professional incompetence, financial irresponsibility, or association with despicable people.

Established legal defenses against accusations of libel or slander fall into several categories. Among other points, they include:

- The person about whom the defamatory statement was made is dead; only the living can be libeled.
- The person about whom the defamatory statement was made is a public figure, not a private individual. While case law makes it much more difficult to libel a public official, the legal determination of just what constitutes a public or private figure often becomes the contentious part of a defamation claim.
- Truth is an absolute defense against charges of libel.

Rather than banking on the prospect of successfully defending a libel claim in court—likely an expensive prospect at best—many archives or repositories with oral history holdings rely on one of several options to protect themselves: editing out offending words in the transcript; masking the identity of the person about whom the libelous statement was made, or sealing offending portions of the interview. Again, sealing portions of an interview or closing it altogether for an extended period of time still would not protect the interview from being opened by court-ordered subpoena; a narrator should be told of this possibility.

ORAL HISTORY ON CAMPUS: DEALING WITH INSTITUTIONAL REVIEW BOARDS

In the mid-1960s, the U.S. Public Health Service began requiring recipients of its biomedical research grants to submit their plans in advance to human subjects protection committees, which came to be known as institutional review boards, or IRBs, which would review them to assure that the rights of individual research subjects would be protected.[4] In the ensuing four decades, expanded federal regulations and expanded perceptions by many campus IRBs of their mission have resulted in a tangled web of regulation, virtually defying generalization, that affects social science and humanities scholars as well as biomedical researchers. To many scholars, they also defy logic and represent a significant threat to academic freedom.[5]

Campus IRBs are legally bound to apply the prior review process only to research funded by one of 17 federal agencies that are parties to the applicable federal rules. As a practical matter, many, but not all, campuses apply the federal standards to all research, regardless of funding source. Furthermore, federal officials have made clear that the federal rules spell out minimum standards for IRB review, and individual campuses are free to make their own rules, with no opportunity for scholars to appeal adverse decisions. Campus IRBs often are dominated by biomedical researchers unfamiliar with scholarly techniques and ethical standards in other academic fields, which has resulted in some legendary IRB excesses:

- A linguist studying language development in a preliterate tribe was ordered by an IRB to have the tribal members read and sign consent forms.
- A Caucasian Ph.D. student was ordered not to interview African-American Ph.D. students for his study of career expectations and ethnicity on

the grounds that such questions might be traumatic.
- An IRB attempted to deny a master's degree to a student who called newspaper executives to ask for publicly available printed materials without first getting IRB approval.[6]

None of those examples specifically relates to oral historians, but efforts by organizations such as the American Historical Association, Oral History Association, and American Association of University Professors to track IRB activities have found numerous instances of IRBs asking oral historians for detailed lists of all questions that will be asked, ordering the destruction of interview recordings, demanding assurances that oral history narrators will remain anonymous, and prohibiting questions that might prove controversial—all of which directly contradict the best practices research standards espoused by ethical oral historians. Moreover, oral historians do not regard their narrators as objects being studied, but rather as collaborators in a joint effort to shed light on people, places, and situations about which the narrator has firsthand knowledge. In an attempt to deal with the inconsistencies and confusion over campus IRB treatment of oral history work, OHA past president Donald A. Ritchie and Linda Shopes, a past president of both the OHA and the AHA, took the lead in the early 2000s to work with the federal Office for Human Research Protection to develop a policy statement articulating how IRBs should treat oral history work. Their work resulted in publication in 2003 of a joint statement asserting that "oral history interviewing, in general, does not meet the regulatory definition of research." Thus it is not subject to the federal regulations "for the protection of human subjects . . . and can be excluded from institutional review board (IRB) oversight."[7]

At issue is the federal definition of "research" as "a systematic investigation, including research development, testing and evaluation, designed to develop or contribute to generalizable knowledge."[8] As Ritchie and Shopes explained, "The type of research encompassed by the regulations involves standard questionnaires with a large sample of individuals who often remain anonymous, not the open-ended interviews with identifiable individuals who give their interviews with 'informed consent' that characterizes oral history."[9]

Many oral historians hoped the policy statement would resolve the inconsistencies in how campus IRBs treated oral history work, but the confusion—and accumulation of horror stories—continued. In June 2006, the American Association of University Professors approved a report of its Committee on Academic Freedom and Tenure, which recommended "that research on autonomous adults whose methodology consists entirely in collecting data by surveys, conducting interviews, or observing behavior in public places, be exempt from the requirement of IRB review—straightforwardly exempt, with no provisos, and no requirement of IRB approval of the exemption."[10] Late in 2007, proposed changes in the federal rules drew dozens of comments, including endorsement of the AAUP position by the American Historical Association and numerous other scholarly organizations and individuals. And in a separate development in December 2007, Columbia University, noting that its Oral History Research Office "administers the world's oldest formal university oral history archive open to the public," issued a policy statement asserting that all oral history projects at the university are to follow the Oral History Association's ethics guidelines and that for the most part such projects do not constitute "human subjects research" and thus are not to be submitted for IRB review, effectively repeating the 2003 policy statement.[11]

So in the absence of unambiguous federal rules and unequivocal treatment by campus IRBs, what are academic oral historians to do? First, assure that plans for an oral history project will withstand ethical scrutiny in accord with the OHA guidelines. With or without IRB review, oral historians must commit themselves to ethical conduct in all their work. Second, work to educate your campus IRB about oral history research methods and about the policy statements outlined here that may influence how it will respond to oral history project proposals. And finally, decide how willing you are to fight for the intellectual integrity of your academic work, regardless of the personal or professional consequences. An IRB that orders an oral historian to destroy recordings, mask the identity of sources, and ask only preapproved questions has turned a project into something unrecognizable as oral history.

ADDITIONAL OBSERVATIONS: ETHICS, ACCESS, AND MONEY

Some archivists and oral history project managers approach the collections management process with a strong conviction that access to the material should be controlled. They argue that researchers or others who want access to oral histories ought to be required to explain their purpose when seeking permission to use or quote from such materials. Attempts to ensure that

oral history materials are used only for purposes the repository deems responsible comes too close to censorship to make others comfortable. But concerns about censorship may take a backseat to the conviction that holders of oral history materials have an ethical obligation to assure that their narrators' words are not used in a way that makes them look foolish or misrepresents them. Some oral historians also believe that controlling use of oral histories is a safeguard to assure that the narrators whose words are used will not be exploited and that they will have a chance to benefit from possible commercial applications of oral history materials.

Commercial applications are, indeed, a reality for many kinds of museum and archival collections, as film and television production companies increasingly turn to such collections for audio, video, and other materials for commercial purposes. Some nonprofit museums and archives, reluctant to be put in the position of subsidizing profit-making companies, have instituted sliding-scale fees for use of such materials. Other repositories have contracts with marketing agencies that enable them to cash in on the value of photographs, interviews, or other elements of their collections for which there is a commercial demand. Such practices, while clearly beneficial to often poorly funded repositories, nonetheless raise questions about how to assure that the narrators themselves—or their heirs—also benefit from the commercial use of their words and voices.

While some project administrators or collections managers advocate controlling use of oral history materials, others see the Internet as a way to increase exponentially the number of users and ease of access to their materials. Many oral history projects have created websites that provide information about their collections, which poses little ethical concern. Others, however, have created websites with full-text transcripts of interviews, audio and video excerpts, and assorted other materials in the collection as well as links to related online resources. Such Internet access can be a researcher's dream, offering connections to collections that might be impossible to visit in person. The immediacy of voices and images online also can create a dramatic impact that captivates website visitors in ways that reading a transcript in an archives reading room cannot.

But ethical issues abound when oral history projects entertain the idea of creating a website as a product of the oral history process. Access to the Internet has become all but universal in the United States, thanks not only to the explosion in personal computers in the home but also to the proliferation of computers and online services available through schools and public libraries. As a result, an oral history collection online is at least theoretically available to hundreds of millions of people, a far cry from the numbers that might visit and use a collection in a library or museum. That vast increase in the size of the potential audience makes it imperative that project coordinators who intend Internet distribution make sure narrators understand the scope of access on the World Wide Web. Many narrators might welcome the prospect; others might not.

Some oral historians worry that the narrator's knowledge that an interview is to be accessible to virtually anyone in the world who has access to a computer will affect the content of the interview itself. Will such widespread access lead narrators to engage in self-censorship to the point of blandness, where potentially valuable but controversial insights will be lost or never revealed? Or will the reverse happen, wherein narrators envisioning a cameo role on a global stage get carried away with their accounts?

Such concerns are not merely theoretical. The proliferation of Internet searching capabilities and heightened concerns in some quarters about national security have raised questions about online publication of oral histories that go beyond concerns about unauthorized profiteering from such material. One oral history collection administrator has reported that a man, originally from India but who had lived in the United States for 30 years, was called twice by FBI investigators who questioned him about his connection to atomic bomb testing in India in the 1990s. He had nothing to do with atomic bomb testing, but, like other Indian Americans interviewed for the oral history project, he was asked about it in the oral history interview. The use of "atomic bomb testing" as a subject keyword in the online finding aid in connection with his name apparently drew the FBI's attention. The administrator removed "atomic bomb testing" as a subject heading in the finding aid, replacing it with the term "current events," which is much less useful to researchers seeking details about the content of the oral history interviews, but which attempts to address concerns that oral history narrators might find themselves being targeted for something they said in interviews published online.[12]

If you decide to publish interview materials online, be especially vigilant in reviewing materials for potentially defamatory language. Protecting against copyright violation also is more difficult with online materials. Oral history websites should contain copyright notices repeated both before and after the transcripts or excerpts to discourage unauthorized use of audio and video materials.

Some oral history practitioners have suggested another option is to renounce copyright claims altogether and assign the materials to the public domain, where all copyrighted materials end up eventually when the copyright terms expire. That idea has not garnered a widespread following in the oral history community, which generally holds to the idea that narrators' words ought not to be considered free for the taking by anyone with commercial interests or an intent to misuse them.

While these legal and ethical concerns might seem to be enough to make would-be oral historians throw in the towel and look for an easier way to spend their energies, don't be discouraged. The legal and ethical framework in which oral historians work has evolved over more than half a century, and it has successfully guided the conduct of untold numbers of oral history interviews. While the rise of the Internet and other digital applications for oral history materials has introduced a new twist to the philosophical and ethical debates over the uses of oral histories, nothing has changed the fundamental ethical requirement that an oral history project be guided by intellectual integrity and a sense of respect for the men and women who are asked to share their stories.

NOTES

1. John A. Neuenschwander. *Oral History and the Law,* 3rd ed. (Carlisle, PA: Oral History Association, 2002).

2. William S. Anderson, editor. *Ballentine's Law Dictionary,* 3rd ed. (Rochester, NY: The Lawyers Co-operative Publishing Company, 1969):321.

3. Neuenschwander discusses defamation issues in considerable detail in *Oral History and the Law*: 17–27.

4. Zachary M. Schrag, "How Talking Became Human Subjects Research: The Federal Regulation of the Social Sciences, 1965–1991," *Journal of Policy History,* forthcoming, available at SSRN: http://ssrn.com/abstract=1124284. In his detailed historical analysis, Schrag notes that many IRB supporters mistakenly believe that application of IRB rules to social science research was a direct result of unethical research and experimentation on human beings beginning in the 1970s. But Schrag asserts that federal regulation of the social sciences actually can be traced to a New Jersey congressman's 1965 concerns about invasion of privacy related to psychological tests on federal employees and applicants for federal jobs. Clearly, however, medical research scandals in the 1970s, particularly a decades-long Public Health Service study

of the effects of syphilis on African American men, sparked renewed congressional attention to medical research ethics, and the present system of elaborate IRB review of federally funded research began to evolve. A detailed discussion of how the policy grew over the years is beyond the scope of this manual, but readers interested in the details will find Schrag's exhaustive account highly informative.

5. The Oral History Association, the American Historical Association, and the American Association of University Professors are among the academic organizations that have taken a leading role in focusing public discussion of the misapplication of rules meant to protect subjects of biomedical research to the work of historians and other humanities and social science scholars. Readers interested in more detailed background than this section provides will find extensive information about IRBs available from these professional associations.

6. "Institutional Review Boards Threaten Scholarly Work," *Oral History Association Newsletter,* Winter 2006:8.

7. "Statement Outlines Oral History Interview Policy," *Oral History Association Newsletter,* Winter 2003:3.

8. Ibid.

9. "Oral History Excluded from IRB Review," *Oral History Association Newsletter,* Winter 2003:1.

10. "Research on Human Subjects: Academic Freedom and the Institutional Review Board (2006)," http://www.aaup.org/AAUP/comm/rep/A/humansubs.htm, accessed June 5, 2008.

11. "Columbia University Articulates IRB Policy," *Oral History Association Newsletter,* Spring 2008:7.

12. Barbara Truesdell, "FBI Use of Oral History Finding Aid," H-Oralhist. http://h-net.msu.edu/cgi-bin/logbrowse, September 28, 2007, accessed June 20, 2008.

CHAPTER 5

Recording Technology

What equipment should you use? Oral historians have faced this question since the first use of mechanical recorders. Equipment decisions are critical steps in the oral history planning process. Misinformation or confusion about equipment basics can stall a project or result in loss of information. The purpose of this chapter is not to recommend one type of equipment or to recommend specific brands or models nor is it meant to recommend or show a bias toward (or against) audio or video. It is, rather, designed to give you the background and tools to make the most beneficial choices for your project.

Given the relatively recent luxury of not only being able to read primary sources but to listen to or view them as well, equipment decisions continue to open up new options for users of oral history materials. Audio-visual archivists, the Oral History Association, and the sources included in the notes at the end of the chapter are excellent sources for updates about recording equipment and media.[1]

A BRIEF HISTORY OF RECORDING EQUIPMENT

Oral historians live with the digital revolution and technological advances. The transition from analog to digital—the digital revolution—has had an impact on oral history projects and collections. It has not changed oral history but has changed "everything about" oral history.[2]

What do we mean by *analog* and *digital*? Both analog and digital recorders transform sound and images into electric current. Analog machines save signals on magnetized media in a continuous pattern as we see or hear them. The recorded signal is a direct analog to sound and image. Digital machines save analog signals as discrete averages of sound and images. Using various software programs and hardware, they take samples, mathematically balance them, and store them as bits of data. The recorded signal is a digitized average of the analog signal.

The necessity of adapting to changes in recording technology is not new. Historically, ethnographers were the first to make field recordings.[3] In the 1890s,

they began by using wax cylinders or discs (hard wax surfaces into which sound grooves were cut). Today these fragile media are in museum collections, and efforts to save the information they contain are ongoing.

Recording technologies that would give rise to oral history began with the invention of the magnetic recorder.[4] The wire recorder, an analog recorder that used steel tape or wire as the magnetized recording medium, was developed in the late 19th and early 20th centuries.[5] Prior to World War II, these machines were somewhat rare and, during the war, most were used by branches of the service. In 1944, Sergeant Forrest Pogue of the Army's Historical Division used one to record accounts of the D-Day invasion.[6] After World War II, wire recorders became more widely available. Allan Nevins of Columbia University, pursuing a pre-war interest, began using them to collect oral histories. In 1948 he founded the Columbia University Oral History Research Office—the first organized program of its kind.[7]

The work of Pogue and Nevins helped establish oral history with its use of recorders to collect interview information. Others quickly saw the potential, including historians at the Bancroft Library at the University of California, Berkeley. Questions about the type of equipment to use, however, surfaced almost immediately. Postwar wire recorders, an improvement over equipment used before World War II, still were bulky and prone to breakdowns.

An early tape recorder, the Magnetophon, was developed in Germany between World War I and World War II. Tape coating experiments at Minnesota Mining and Manufacturing Company (now 3M) began in 1944. Discovery of several Magnetophons in Frankfurt, Germany, near the end of World War II furthered the work. These were large pieces of analog equipment that used a blank supply tape on an open reel to record sound as it threaded to a take-up reel. Portable, self-contained reel-to-reel recorders appeared in 1951. Audiocassettes—audiotapes housed in plastic cases containing both the supply and take-up reels—went on the market in 1963. Analog recorders were universal, meaning any reel-to-reel or cassette recording could be played on any reel-to-reel or cassette equipment.

Digital technology—the use of discrete numerical values to represent data or information read by a computer—appeared in the early 1980s. Recording media for digital technology have included the Digital Audio Tape (DAT), compact discs (CDs), flash drives, and sound cards, among many options.[8]

Developments in video recording technology moved as fast as the audio recording field. Ampex began work on videotape and a videotape recorder in 1951. The first home videotape recorder was marketed in 1963. The first videocassette, the 3/4-inch U-Matic, was introduced in 1969 and became the world standard for videocassettes. The first consumer video camcorder (its name is a contraction of *camera* and *recorder*) was introduced by Sony in 1980. The introduction of digital video brought additional variety to the market. The major medium was the DVD (Digital Versatile Disc, also known as Digital Video Disc), for which commercial standards were agreed to in 1995. Blu-ray Discs (BD), which use blue-violet laser to write and read data, and high-definition (HD), which hit the market in 1998 with increased quality and resolution, are the next generation of digital video media.

EQUIPMENT CHOICES AS PART
OF THE ORAL HISTORY PLANNING PROCESS

As you can see from this brief overview of the evolution of recording formats, the one constant in recording equipment history is change. Formats are created and abandoned, and at any one time a number of different formats are available. Understanding the range of equipment types will help you make the best decision for a project.

This doesn't mean oral historians must be experts in recording technology. A working knowledge of the basics outlined in this chapter will help guide project decisions. Depending on your level of interest or expertise, you also may want to enlist help from a person with a strong background in computers and recording technology. But if you do, remember that ideally anyone you look to for advice should understand, or be willing to learn about, the specific recording needs of oral history, especially the need for continuing access to the full interview as given and for maximizing longevity and retrievability of the original recording.

Sources of information about recording equipment are mentioned throughout the chapter. Archivists and librarians, the Oral History Association and its list-server, and the referenced websites all are excellent resources and good places to turn for the most up-to-date oral history equipment information.

Basic Recommendations

Where to start? Think first about several basic recommendations:

- use the best-quality recording equipment you can afford
- use high-quality external microphones
- use the highest-quality connecting cables
- use headphones

Recordings that maintain long-term sound quality and accessibility are the goal of oral history practitioners. The use of production-quality recorders is recommended whenever possible. High-quality external microphones, another item on the above list, circumvent built-in recorder microphones and maximize recording quality. They provide the clearest and cleanest sound. High-quality connecting cables also help maximize recording or sound quality. Headphones allow the interviewer to monitor the sound as the interview is being recorded, thus helping avoid loss of the interview information.

Production and Archival Quality

Oral historians work with production-quality and archival-quality standards. Production quality, also described as broadcast quality, is a recording equipment standard. The specifications refer to the most recent commercial recording guidelines.

Archival quality refers to the following:

- The approximate length of time the production-quality recording technology is expected to last
- The natural lifespan of the media
- The length of time playback equipment will be available[9]

Let's review each of the archival standards. The first, the approximate length of time the high-quality or production-quality recording technology is expected to last, is, at least ideally, an indication of stability and long-term access. If the recording equipment is not universal—meaning any recording can be played on any equipment—the recording and playback technology should at least be as widely available as possible. And equipment using proprietary technology—in which recording and playback options are restricted by software or hardware requirements and are linked to specific manufacturers—should be well documented.

The natural lifespan of the media is another standard. This refers to the amount of time the recording is salvageable and retrievable. Reel-to-reel tapes were the recording and archival standard for four decades. With proper care and access to a recorder, they can be played for decades after an interview session. Digital interviews are recorded and stored in a variety of ways. The general lifespan of each has yet to be determined, although migration (transfer of information to the latest format) could extend accessibility.

Rapid technological change makes it important to be aware of the length of time playback equipment is available. Obsolete playback technology can make oral history recordings inaccessible.

BASIC USE FACTORS

The next step is to consider basic use factors. They are:

- cost
- project goals
- audio and video
- project repositories

Cost

Recording equipment costs vary considerably. Although it may be tempting to save money on less expensive options, look carefully at equipment specifications before making a decision. Does the recorder have a removable sound card? This will allow for flexibility in long-term use. Does it have the option to record in unreduced sound, also referred to as uncompressed sound, a basic standard for digital oral history recordings? Are there proprietary factors in the software that can inhibit access to the recordings, either in the short term or the long term?

What about the cost of the recording media? Recording media, such as removable sound cards, are an extra expense to be factored into equipment costs. The media or server space needed to store the interview is another cost factor. While not a direct recording equipment cost, it is an item to consider when developing a budget for purchasing recorders.

Project Goals

The second consideration involves project goals. What are the purposes of the project and how and where will the recordings be used? Project directors will want to think about not only short-term access and use but ac-

cess over decades. Will recordings be in formats that can continue to be accessible as the digital revolution races along? In what ways can your choice of equipment help maximize this possibility?

Ease of use in the interview setting is another factor. How easy is the equipment to use? How sturdy is it? Will it hold up through multiple users in a variety of interview settings and conditions?

Audio and Video

Here, your decision will be based on the project budget, project goals, type and availability of equipment, and narrator preferences. Each of these factors is important. Video cameras have come down in price and can record in uncontrolled environments, although the video will be only as good as the lighting and environment in which it is made. Because video combines audio recording with visual images, it is a more complex medium and its use can require more planning. Carefully check options, including controlled environment needs such as equipment, lights, deflectors, and trained personnel.

Audio and Video

Audio

Can be less costly

More flexibility in interview setting

Depending on the type of equipment, may allow for stronger interviewer-narrator bonding

Can be less intrusive

Video

Can be more costly

Depending on type of equipment, can involve additional personnel

More complex interview setting needs

Provides access to visual materials, such as photographs, artifacts, and physical settings

Collects nonverbal information such as gestures and facial expressions

---

Video equipment should be used by someone trained to handle the added technical elements that are part of a successful oral history video recording. Depending on the situation and the type of video equipment used, this can mean added expense. If you don't have access to trained personnel for your project, a professional camera operator can provide expertise, including knowledge about the interview environment, types of equipment, lenses, lighting, sound, interview setting, retrievability options, and the additional technical details that affect the quality of the recording.

Project directors sometimes expect the interviewer to operate the camera. Care should be taken here, however, for each job—interviewer and camera operator—requires full-time concentration to make the most of the interview. An experienced interviewer may find using a digital video camera allows one person to do it all, but planners should consider the challenges associated with expecting one person to be both the interviewer and videographer.

Recorders are oral history practitioners' tools. When thinking about using video equipment, consider the following:

- What is the purpose of video? Is access to the context that video provides integral to understanding the narrator's story?
- What is the context the video will provide? Will it add visual information to the interview? If so, what type? How does the visual information strengthen the narrator's story? How does it contribute to the project purposes? Is the visual element needed to document the narrator's expressions and body language? How important is this to understanding the interview information and why?
- Does the visual information document background footage that can be shot as a second interview after the initial audio recording?
- What are the short-term and long-term uses of the video information? Is it produced for immediate programming needs? Oral history guidelines stipulate that original recordings, audio and video, be kept intact and programming be done with copies. How does this affect the decision to use video?
- Will the project use production-quality video recording equipment? As with audio equipment, some video equipment may produce a recording that sounds and looks good in the short run, but may not be sustainable in the long term.
- What types of media will be used, and how accessible and retrievable will the interview information be, short term and long term? Are there media types that can maximize accessi-

bility and retrievability? If so, how available are they to the project?
- What are the video preservation needs? What are the unreduced (uncompressed) storage needs for video data files? What are plans for ongoing access to the video information?

Careful consideration of the impact on narrator and interviewer-narrator interaction is another part of the planning process. Just because video is available does not mean it must be used or even that it should be used. Audio-only interviews were the recording standard for decades, and they continue to have value. Questions to ask about the impact of video on the interview participants include:

- Who will be in charge of the video interview? Is it the interviewer? Is it the videographer? What impact will this have on interview participants?
- Is the equipment too intrusive? Interviews can be intense and the presence of recording equipment may be unsettling. What impact could this have on the use of video? What impact could video have on the interview information? What impact could video have on the narrator? What impact could video have on the interviewer?
- How will the interviewer and narrator be perceived on camera? If the narrator is nervous will this affect the credibility of the information presented? How important a consideration is this for the project?
- Will the video materials stereotype the narrator or other interview participants or create biases in any way?
- What are the narrator's wishes for the interview? Are there narrators whose information may be lost because of reticence to go on camera? Are there narrators who may refuse to participate in the project because they are uncomfortable just being in front of the camera? What impact will that have on the project?[10]
- What are the needs of the project, short-term and long-term? Sometimes video is necessary. Interviews done in sign language are a good example. Video interviews also document other nonverbal communications, such as gestures, facial expressions, body language, and complex expressions that are difficult to

translate into words. They collect information that cannot be communicated in an audio interview.

Video has other advantages. Although most oral history interviews are conducted one-on-one, video also is useful if an interview involves more than one narrator since it makes it easier to see who is saying what. It also is useful if the narrator has items such as photographs or artifacts that visually enhance the interview. And video can provide material for possible exhibit or Internet uses, although development of useful footage also involves careful planning.

There are options for combining audio and video. First recording an audio interview and then working with the narrator to record visual images that supplement or complement it can be very effective. This allows projects to include video recording techniques while not relying exclusively on them. For example, 32 narrators were recorded through the Minnesota Historical Society's Minnesota Environmental Issues Oral History Project. After completing these interviews, project director James E. Fogerty followed up with video interviews with four narrators, each at a location that illustrated information given during the narrator's audio interview. Through careful planning for the video in a follow-up interview, Fogerty was able to gather additional information in a setting that maximized the use of visual images.

We are an increasingly visual culture. Often the decision by oral history project leaders is to automatically assume the use of video. Many oral historians believe that what it brings to a project far outweighs anything else. As with all oral history planning process steps, however, care and caution are watchwords. Do not let technology drive the equipment planning process. Audio and video recording options are tools for oral historians. Use the format that will best serve the purposes of a project.

Project Repositories
Before making equipment decisions, talk with the manager of the repository where your collection ultimately will reside.[11] Most repositories, be they small and volunteer-run or large multifaceted organizations, have format requirements. Repositories generally will not accept formats they cannot support over the long term. Don't forget to ask what kinds of recording equipment and media your repository will accept and continue to support. Working with an archivist or other repository personnel can save time and money.

> Check with your repository for format requirements or guidelines when selecting equipment.

RECORDERS, MEDIA, AND ACCESSORIES

When you have examined your options based on the above guidelines, the next step is to look at various types of recording equipment. The basic equipment questions you will want to ask when planning an oral history project involve:

- Recorders
- Microphones, headphones, and cables
- Media

Recorders
The most important equipment issue for oral historians to consider is quality of the recording. Production-quality equipment is the ideal, but it may not always be available. Oral historians can help determine whether recording equipment will fill a project's needs by examining sound and sound reduction specifications. The quality of digital sound is measured in sampling rate and bit depth.[12] Sampling rate is the number of sound samples taken per second. The more samples, the better quality the sound. A standard CD sampling rate is 44,100/second, written as 44.1 kHz. Bit depth is the number of bits of sound used to encode a sound file. The more bits, the more accurate the sound. A standard CD has 16 bits.

> When choosing recording equipment, check current standards and equipment specifications. Oral historians work in unreduced sound and formats, also known as uncompressed sound and formats, with specified sampling rates and bit depths.

Most digital recorders have the option to reduce the data—put it into a more compact form by discarding anything the recorder identifies as redundant. Unreduced data is represented in file format as WAVE and Broadcast Wave Format (waveform sound files, identified by the .wav or .bwf file extension) for PC computers and AIFF (.aif or .aiff file extension) for Macintosh users. Check the recorder's user handbook for the sampling rate, bit depth, and file extension as a guide to its sound quality.

When sound is reduced, access to compacted materials comes through perceptual coding (a codec or algorithm that processes digital files) that works with the computer operating system. This reduces the data representing the sequence of recorded signals, encoding (translating recorded signals into digital format) differences between frames, and discarding similarities. Codecs vary, depending on what they are used for, and are identified by the file extension. "Lossy" codecs, which process greatly reduced audio and video digital signals, are common because they can produce smaller files while retaining the data basics; users know the human mind can fill in any minor blanks.[13] Two of the more widely known are Jpeg and Mpeg (file extensions are .jpeg and .mpeg). Each has a reduction ratio (the size of the original unreduced data file divided by the size of its reduced version) that expresses the degree to which reduction has occurred. When used to reduce sound, lossy codecs do not allow restoration of the data to its original acoustic condition.

Lossless codecs also are an option for audio digital recordings. Lossless codecs reduce data, but, unlike lossy codecs, do not discard data in the process. With lossless codecs, full sound can be restored evenly across the range from high to low.[14] Examples of lossless codecs are pulse code modulation (PCM) for .aif/.aiff and .wav and linear pulse code modulation (LPCM) for .bwf.

Default settings on recorders usually are in lossy codecs. The recorder's handbook should include a process for reformatting into an unreduced format. An example of production- and archival-quality digital equipment recording standards is .wav or .bwf (unreduced) format, PCM or linear PCM (lossless codec), 16–24 bits, sampled at 44.1–48 kHz.[15] Check with archives, historical organizations, the Society of American Archivists, or the Oral History Association for information about the most current standards and specifications.

Digital audio recording equipment should have the following basic features: two external microphone jacks, a display window that shows recorder functions, manual volume control, a headphone jack, the option to record in unreduced (uncompressed) sound, a removable memory or sound card, USB interface, on/off switch, and an AC adapter. Video recorders should have the following features at a minimum: a professional-quality zoom lens, the ability to accommodate professional-

quality microphones preferably with xlr connections, an option for recording on standard play (SP) or in unreduced format, manual volume control, a removable sound or memory card, USB interface, and on/off switch.[16] Additional equipment for video interviews can include: sound mixer, light stands and lamps, monitor (to review the video as it will look), edit controller, and several editing VCRs.[17] Most video recorders have just one microphone jack, but a Y-cable or splitter allows you to plug two microphones into one jack.

Microphones, Headphones, and Cables

A high-quality external microphone allows future listeners to clearly hear the interviewer and the narrator (that is, the full structure of the interview) without the distraction of motor noise from the recorder. Make sure the microphone is insulated to prevent picking up extra noise when touched. The options are lavalieres—small microphones clipped to the clothing—or microphones that use a stand or a pad.

Microphones come in two types, condenser or dynamic. A condenser translates acoustical signals into electrical ones using a variable capacitor (a voltage-storing component) that requires a battery. A dynamic translates acoustical signals into electrical ones using a coil moving in a magnetic field. It generates its own electric current and does not need a battery.

Microphones have several sound pickup patterns. Omnidirectional patterns pick up all sound in a field around the microphone. Cardioid microphones pick up sound predominantly from the direction in which the microphone is pointed in a heart-shaped pattern. Unidirectional microphones pick up sound from one direction only.

Oral historians use either dynamic directional lavaliere microphones—one for each participant in an interview—or one dynamic omnidirectional microphone placed to pick up everyone's voices. Either of these options will clearly pick up all voices in an interview.

> Use one omnidirectional microphone or directional lavaliere microphones to pick up the narrator's and interviewer's voices.

When choosing a microphone, make sure it is compatible with the recorder. If using a microphone that needs a stand, it is essential to use a sturdy, stable microphone stand that allows the interviewer to position the microphone for optimum sound recording. These vary from free-standing models to those that clamp on to a flat surface to soft foam pads made especially to hold a microphone. As with all equipment decisions, if you have questions, contact an expert familiar with voice recording for advice.

Equipment accessories also are important. Headphones permit the interviewer to monitor sound and resolve any audio problems that develop during the interview. Good cables help make good-quality sound. Make sure cables and connectors between the microphone and recording equipment are shielded (the conductors are wrapped) to reduce interference. Use coaxial cables (with inner and outer conductors) for video recording. Cables should allow for maximum flexibility in positioning the recorder and microphone.

Media

Media are another equipment factor to consider. As with types of recording equipment, each has specific characteristics. Many digital audio recorders capture the sound or video on a memory card, also called a flash memory card. These are solid state data-storage devices. The number of megabytes (MB) and gigabytes (GB) of storage space each has will help determine its usefulness in recording an oral history interview in an unreduced format. The file size of an unreduced 60-minute interview recorded in stereo at 16 bits with a sample rate of 44.1–48 kHz is 600–800 MBs. The file size of an unreduced 60-minute interview recorded in stereo at 24 bits with a sample rate of 96 kHz is 1.980 GBs.[18]

Storage

Unlike analog, digital recordings are not stored on the media used to record the interview. Equipment decisions should include a plan for electronic storage of interview data files. This covers transferring interview files to a server or hard drive, or to a compact disc (CD) as a user or backup copy. When storing electronic files, the best approach is to make multiple copies on multiple pieces of equipment and media. Oral historian Doug Boyd advises, "Make multiple copies in multiple formats and keep them in multiple places."[19]

A server environment that provides regular backups and automatic checks for monitoring and maintaining data file integrity (checking for data file corruption) is an optimum storage option. An external hard drive can be a backup for a server environment or it can be used as primary storage if a server environment is not available. Look for an external hard drive that provides options for automatically monitoring data files to make future conversions and migrations as easy as possible.[20] A 60-minute, unreduced 16 bit/44.1 kHz file takes up between 600 and 800 megabytes of space while a reduced lossy codec file, such as mpeg, takes up 56.4.megabytes.[21] A lossless codec will reduce the original file to about half its unreduced size.[22]

CDs are manufactured for short-term playback rather than long-term storage. They can provide user access to interview data files and sometimes are used as a secondary backup system, although volatility and threat of file loss are factors in this decision. Migration of information on CDs also is very labor intensive.

Gold CDs made with phthalocyanine dye and a gold reflective layer are less volatile than standard CDs. The gold provides a protective, chemically inert outer layer that may help stabilize the CD. As a general guideline, if CDs are part of the user access or storage plan, use 74minute/650MB gold CD-Rs.[23] Do not use adhesive labels and do not write on the CD surfaces. Use a water-based, permanent pen and write identifying information on the plastic inner part of the CD. Store the CDs in polypropylene cases and acid-free boxes.[24] Use Mylar sleeves if needed.

Video storage is more complex—an added factor when considering when and how to record in video. An hour of video recording can require as much as 30 GB of server space. Because of file size and technical needs, archival storage of uncompressed video data files can be very expensive, as can the playback equipment needed to access the files.[25] Look for server space that provides regular backups and automatic checks for monitoring and maintaining data file integrity. If an external hard drive can be incorporated into a storage plan, use one that will automatically monitor data files and make future conversions and migrations as easy as possible.[26]

DVDs face the same volatility and loss risks as CDs. Media obsolescence also is a factor.[27] Gold DVDs provide user access to data files and sometimes are used as backup storage. When using gold DVDs, look for those made with the same process as gold CDs. Follow the same procedures for marking and storage.

Transcribing Equipment

Transcribing guidelines are covered in the planning and processing chapters. Transcribing, however, also involves equipment that uses either analog tapes or digital data files. Analog transcribing equipment has earpieces or headsets, foot pedals, and tape speed controls. Digital transcribing equipment uses headsets, foot pedals, and computer software that works in .wav files.[28]

Recording Equipment and Media Not Recommended for Oral History Use

What about equipment not recommended for use by oral history practitioners? This section is not meant as a heavy-handed set of rules, but as a guide to maximize full accessibility and long-term retrievability of oral history information.

Oral history projects generally do not need equipment made for high-end music recording, but you can maximize the life and use of the interviews with the best voice and/or visual production-quality recorders you can find. Over-the-counter audio recorders manufactured for home use, while perhaps sounding good at the time of the initial recording, rarely meet oral history standards. Neither do video recorders manufactured for home use. They do not record to production-quality standards and the long-term viability and retrievability of the recorded information is unproven. Doug Boyd advises, "If you can buy recording equipment in an office supply store, typically it should not be used in an oral history interview."[29]

If you are using analog recorders, avoid mini-cassettes. The quality of the recording cannot be sustained. Also avoid voice-activated recorders. They shut down when people are not talking, omitting pauses in the interview that can be important to understanding its context. Each stop and start also inserts a breaking sound on the tape that mars overall quality.

Some people choose to record with computer laptops. Few archivists recommend this practice, but if you use a laptop, have an expert check the hardware setup for optimum recording viability. MP3 players have recording functions added to them, but they are not ideal for oral history use from a long-term preservation standpoint. And, regardless of the type of recorder, it is helpful to avoid proprietary formats whenever possible because of long-term software and hardware accessibility issues.

The rapid equipment and media evolution of the digital age has led to the relatively rapid appearance and disappearance of some items. Ideally, try to use equipment and media that meet the archival standards described at the beginning of this chapter. Digital minidiscs, for example, were commercially popular, but quickly disappeared from store shelves. They have been surpassed by other media.

The information in this chapter is designed to help you think through some basic equipment and media decisions. Always check for the most up-to-date information available. Consult archivists, the oral history listserver, the Oral History Association, the Society of American Archivists, and the sources listed at the end of this chapter. Equipment issues and recommendations are a moving target. Your project and your interviews will benefit from the most current information you can find.

WHAT OTHER QUESTIONS CAN HELP GUIDE EQUIPMENT DECISIONS FOR YOUR PROJECT?

Does the equipment conform to national and international standards regarding basic specifications, interchangeability, and compatibility among brands? Analog audio recorders are universal, meaning any recording can be played on any piece of equipment regardless of brand. This is not always true for digital recorders, hence the importance of this question.

Who will be doing the interviewing and who will train interviewers to use the equipment? Thorough interviewer training on recording equipment is essential. Nothing is worse than sending someone out on an interview only to find that inexperience with the equipment results in either a poor-quality product or complete loss of the information. Inexperienced or untrained interviewers also pay more attention to the equipment than to the narrator, which can lower the quality of the interview. Choose equipment that interviewers can learn to use with confidence.

Who is available for help and equipment/media support? Interviewer training does not completely solve the equipment use issue. Whether using volunteers, graduate assistants, or interviewers with many years' experience, there are times when it is helpful to have someone to turn to with questions about use of the equipment. Knowing your community and the kinds of support and expertise available for various types of recorders can help you choose equipment best suited to your needs.

What are the interviewing conditions? Conditions at the interview setting can affect your equipment decisions. What are the conditions in which the interviewers will be operating, and what type of equipment is best suited to these situations? Given that interviewers may not always have access to electricity and other amenities, how well does the equipment operate on batteries? How rugged is it, and how well does it perform in a variety of situations?

What factors can cause loss of recorded signal and how often does this occur? One of the greatest fears of oral historians is to find out, too late, that the great interview just completed didn't record because of equipment problems. It is always helpful to ask how to identify factors leading to possible equipment or media recording malfunctions. You will also want to ask, should the worst happen, how much information lost due to malfunctioning equipment or media you can expect to retrieve with the equipment you want to use, how this is done, what the cost of doing it is, and who is available to do it.

Including video in an oral history project is another critical equipment decision. Here are some questions to help guide you. Answers to these equipment planning questions can help you make your decision.

What is your project budget and how will video enhance the final result?

Video can be expensive. As with audio, the use of production-quality equipment—the camera, the external microphones, and media—is the oral history standard. How can you best maximize project resources? If limited resources exist, where and how will video fit best? What is most useful for your project and why? Does every interview need to be recorded in video? Why or why not? Could an interview benefit from combining audio and selected video recordings, using video to complement or supplement the audio where it is most useful?

Who and what will be on video? Will video provide talking heads, or will it be used to provide a visual element that complements or provides additional background to the information being collected? If video provides talking heads, how will this further the goals of your project? How will your project benefit from the use of video, and how is this reconciled with overall needs and budget resources?

Are camera operators or videographers available if needed to make video recordings and how accessible are they to your project? What is their experience with oral history? What is the cost of using them?

Who will conduct the video interviews and what experience does this person have with video oral history? Just as audio interviews should be researched and organized, video interviews must be carefully planned. Video interviews can involve one or more equipment operators or the interviewer working alone. Regardless, the interviewer is in charge of the interview and, working with the camera operator, makes final decisions on set, lighting, and camera angles.

What are the possible needs at the recording site, such as special lenses, lighting, microphones, cables and acces- sories, and necessary power sources? If these are not readily available, how can you provide for each?

How will a video recording session affect the narrator and interviewer? It is helpful to think about the presence of video equipment and whether it will distract the narrator, preventing successful interaction between interviewer and narrator during the interview. It is also helpful to be aware of possible effects of video recording equipment on the interviewer and to incorporate video interviewing techniques into interviewer training sessions whenever video will be used.

What are the recording conditions for use of video? If the interview is to be recorded outdoors, do you know how this will affect the recording? How does this contrast with the use of a studio, the narrator's home or place of business, or other indoor settings? It is helpful to find out how to maintain production-quality audio and video standards in each setting. What will result in video that furthers project goals?

What are the wishes of the narrators? Do the narrators understand they will be on video? Do they understand how the project plans to use the video? Do they understand there can be additional uses of the video in the future? Do they agree to be on video under these circumstances?

Will video be useful for future projects, and is this a determining factor for your project? You may want to think about the possible future uses of video interviews and then decide if meeting undefined future needs is part of your project goal or purpose.

WHAT ABOUT PLANNED ACCESS AND RETRIEVABILITY OF INTERVIEW MATERIALS?

Access questions are major factors to consider when developing a project and choosing equipment. This becomes especially obvious when requests to use interview materials for projects, such as museum exhibits or websites, begin to come in. Although the fundamental purpose of oral history is to collect primary-source material documenting firsthand information, project coordinators increasingly consider its use in audio or video products as an important project outcome.

Key access questions relate to potential uses of the materials, the choice of repository, and interview processing techniques. Oral history projects typically record interviews for both immediate and long-term use, although immediate use, such as a publication, audiovisual program, or museum exhibit, can drive project development. With this in mind, the type of project and the need to quickly and easily gain access to oral history materials become factors in choosing equipment. These questions can help guide the planning process.

Who will be responsible for the oral history collection at the repository? What experience do repository personnel have in handling oral history materials and in handling your formats? Oral history collections need specialized care. Does the repository have the resources to care for the kinds of formats you want to use? Does the repository recommend specific formats?

How many interviews will be recorded, and what are the equipment, media, and estimated server space needs for preserving the recorded information? What about the use of external hard drives? Digitally recorded interviews are stored on server storage space or on external hard drives. It may take several external hard drives to hold copies of interviews. When using external hard drives to store or back up multiple copies of interviews, can you keep the hard drives in separate locations that provide adequate storage conditions? See above for sizes of unreduced files to determine the amount of server space and the size and number of external hard drives needed for interview data file storage.

What is the plan for technological change? What about backup strategies? Oral history project leaders will want to determine a repository's practices for retaining access to the interview materials.

What equipment does the repository keep on hand to play tapes or discs when needed? What software and hardware systems does the digital equipment use? What are the repository's policies for maintaining equipment and software and hardware systems that continue to provide access to the recordings?

Who is available to provide equipment maintenance needed for accessibility to the interview information? It is helpful to know about the types of maintenance the equipment needs, how it should be done, what is most likely to need repairing, and what the possible repair costs can be. Librarians and school audio-visual staff can be helpful sources of information on equipment maintenance and repair track records.

What are the plans for making copies of the interviews and for keeping the originals as the preservation masters? What equipment is available for copying? What medium will interviews be copied onto and why? What are the resources for making user copies of the material?

Who will be processing the information in the interview, and what equipment is available for this purpose? What type of processing (developing a transcript, a recording abstract) will be done, and what types of processing equipment are needed? What medium should materials be in for processing? What will it take to put the recorded interview material into a format for processing? If full transcripts are to be made (important for both audio and video interviews), access to the contents of the interview probably will be ongoing. But if you decide to rely only on a recording abstract, how will continued access to the spoken information be maintained?

How do you plan to use information from the interviews? While collecting oral history will add primary-source material to repositories, oral history interviews often are used to provide material for museum exhibits, radio and television programs, websites, and written materials, among many other uses. What are some possible uses of the interviews beyond their status as primary-source documents? What formats would make them more useful, and what kinds of personnel, equipment, and budget would be needed to put the interviews into these formats?

Do you have plans to put project materials on the Internet or on digital TV? You may be interested in streaming. Material on the Internet also can easily be moved to digital TV. Keeping in mind the Internet does not replace the need for a permanent repository for project materials, what formats are needed for website development? What are your reasons for putting project information on the World Wide Web, and how do they further overall project development? What are the steps and costs needed to put project materials into a format for use on the World Wide Web? How do Web-related needs affect other access issues?

WHAT ABOUT RECORDING TECHNOLOGY AND LONG-TERM SALVAGING OF RECORDINGS?

Although it is sometimes difficult to think about the needs of researchers and others well into the future, the purpose of oral history is to collect and preserve information that could otherwise be lost. Once collected, this primary-source material is as important and unique as a diary or as letters dating back hundreds of years. Just as people today still read first-person accounts about life on the Overland Trail in diaries and letters written by 19th-century travelers, people in the future will turn to oral histories to learn from the information they contain. Oral history materials also are being sought more often for audio or video uses beyond those designed into the project. Although the lifespan of the recordings is finite, adherence to production and archival standards whenever possible will help you maximize accessibility to the recorded interviews.

This step in equipment planning is one of the most important but it can also be one of the most difficult and confusing. Bruce Bruemmer pointed out in a 1991 *American Archivist* article that "oral historians are [often] producers, not curators."[30] This dilemma is reflected in what may be referred to as the contradictory needs of historic records maintenance. Paul Eisloeffel notes that archivists are responsible for the long-term care of records and media created for a more immediate or very different purpose. The challenge is in providing long-term care and maintenance of materials created in a variety of formats using a variety of media, each of which has its own preservation needs. This is increasingly an issue when oral historians have a variety of equipment types, software and hardware systems, and media from which to choose.

As software, hardware, and media change and are updated, archivists and others owning oral history materials will be faced with maintaining access to the information in the most up-to-date formats. Many institutions regularly transfer materials to newer formats. The transfer processes are called digitizing (transferring analog to digital), refreshing (recreating files on new software-hardware systems), reformatting (moving files to software-hardware systems with different specifications), and migrating (moving data between media). Archivists recommend that digitized items be transferred to the latest formats every five years to keep up with changes in technology.

As you look at various types of recording equipment and media, consider these long-term access issues for oral history materials:

Will analog recordings be digitized? Digitization should be done according to the most up-to-date technological standards available. If an original recording is in analog format, that is the archival master. After digitizing, it should be retained in the collections. Digitization is a process that puts the recording into a different format; never use it as a reason for discarding the archival master.[31]

What are the equipment, media, and estimated server space needs for preserving the recorded information? What is the plan for technological change? What about backup strategies? Ask repository personnel these questions to help determine options for ongoing retrievability. As noted above, some oral history projects use multiple external hard drives as backups.

What about equipment obsolescence? What happens when the equipment needed to play the recordings is no longer available or the parts needed to maintain existing out-of-date equipment are no longer available?

What plans does the repository have to hold onto and maintain out-of-date equipment to provide access to recordings for the lifespan of the media? This is as true for continued access to analog in reel-to-reel or cassette formats as it is for CDs, sound cards, and interviews stored on servers.

What about format obsolescence? Is the software and hardware you are using proprietary (unavailable for use without permission from the manufacturer) or is it open and standard? What happens when the software and hardware systems you are using are no longer available? How will this affect access? What are the plans for regularly upgrading software and hardware access systems?

Are the equipment and media backward compatible and, if so, for how many generations? Backward compatibility, also called downward compatibility, refers to the ability to use data and files created with earlier technologies on new equipment and media. For instance, will new technology accept and allow access to materials created with earlier versions of software? Backward compatibility reduces the need to start over when technology is upgraded.

Are the equipment and media forward compatible? Forward compatibility, also called upward compatibility, refers to planning for access to data and files created with earlier technologies on future upgrades.

Is a lossy or lossless codec needed to read digitally recorded information? What do you know about its ability to provide ongoing access to the materials?

How is the interview information stored? Data reduction is a factor for oral historians because unreduced files are large, a consideration when storing large numbers of interviews. What about the availability of server space for long-term storage of the interviews? What about additional storage options? What is available and what is the lifespan for maintaining access to the interviews?

What are the repository's policies for long-term access to oral history materials (digital and analog, audio and video) in its collections? As software and hardware technology changes, how will the repository handle ongoing access? Realizing analog is less complex than digital but that both have specific archival needs, what are the policies for long-term access to the sound archives?

If the repository has collections in several digital formats, what are its policies for maintaining access to each? Does it have collections in the various formats? What are staff and budget priorities for maintaining access? What are its policies and priorities for standardizing formats?

What are staff and budget priorities for care of analog and digital materials, including ongoing access to refreshment technology, commitment to refreshing collections, and number of copies made? It is difficult to determine future budget commitments and needs, but a thorough discussion of these issues can be helpful.

What about sound quality throughout the migration process? Although the data reduction process normally runs smoothly, with too much reduction or an incorrect ratio, artifacts (sounds or images that shouldn't be there) can appear and, if they do, they can permanently affect the quality of the digitized materials. You will also want to ask about the effects of data reduction on multiple copies made over time.

What are the most recent archival staff recommendations regarding long-term stability of your chosen format (digital and analog)? This information may be obtained through local historical organizations, the media archivist at your state historical society, and the Oral History Association.

FINAL RECOMMENDATIONS

Deciding what equipment to use can be a thorny issue for oral historians. While the above discussion can help you make an informed decision about your interview needs as well as accessibility and retrievability of the recordings, keep in mind that this discussion highlights ideal choices. Projects rarely have the funding to acquire the full assortment of equipment and media covered here. When funding needs are an issue, the first priority for many projects is acquiring the best recording equipment they can afford along with a high-quality microphone and high-quality cables.

The final suggestion is: Always do your homework. The resources listed in this chapter are good places to start. You may find that the newest technology does not fit your needs or it may not be supported by your repository. If your budget is tight, you may find that equipment can be donated or loaned. Schools, two- and four-year colleges, and universities often have media centers with good recording equipment that can be sources of help or support. And always remember that although recording technology changes rapidly, informed and thoughtful equipment decisions during the oral history planning process enhance the immediate and long-term accessibility, uses, and retrievability of your oral history recordings.

> Always do your homework when deciding on equipment for your oral history project.

NOTES

1. Because of rapidly changing technology, equipment specifications can change quickly. For up-to-date oral history technology information, see the work of Doug Boyd at the University of Kentucky and Jill Koelling at the Collaborative Digitization Program, Denver, Colorado. See also Andy Kolovos, "Field Recording in the Digital Age" at the Vermont Folklife Center, http://www.vermontfolklife center.org/archive/res_audioequip.htm, accessed December 11, 2007.

2. Doug Boyd, "Oral History and Technology," presentation at "The Start of Something New," University of Wisconsin–Madison Oral History Day Program, April 14, 2008.

3. Information on the history of technology is from David Morton, *Off the Record: The Technology and Culture of Sound Recording in America* (New Brunswick, NJ: Rutgers University Press, 2000) and Steven E. Schoenherr, "Recording Technology History," notes revised July 6, 2005. http://history.sandiego.edu/GEN/recording/notes.html, accessed December 31, 2008.

4. Definitions for technical terms in this chapter are from Brad Hansen, *The Dictionary of Computing and Digital Media: Terms & Acronyms* (Wilsonville, OR: ABF Content, 1999).

5. "Recording History: The History of Recording Technology," http://www.recording-history.org/HTML/wire7.php, accessed October 5, 2008.

6. Donald A. Ritchie, "Remembering Forrest Pogue," *Oral History Association Newsletter*, Winter 1997:7.

7. For more information, see Rebecca Sharpless, "The History of Oral History" in *Handbook of Oral History* by Thomas L. Charlton, Lois E. Myers, and Rebecca Sharpless, eds. (Lanham, MD: AltaMira Press, 2006):19–42.

8. *Disc* is sometimes spelled *disk*. We have chosen the first spelling as the more common.

9. Robyn Russell, "Archival Considerations for Librarians and Oral Historians," *Oral History Association Newsletter*, Spring 2004:4–5.

10. Issues about use of video in oral history can parallel those related to use of cameras in courtrooms. See "Cameras in the Courtroom" in Justice in Society, http://justiceinsociety.blogspot.com/2007/11/cameras-in-courtroom.html, accessed September 11, 2008. "The Pros and Cons of Television in the Courtroom" by Joyce M. Cossin, http://www.wcu.edu/WebFiles/PDFs/PSYCossin-j-8-03.pdf, accessed September 11, 2008.

11. For an example of standards, see Dietrich Schüller, *IASA-TC 03 und 04: Standards Related to the Long-Term*

Preservation and Digitisation of Sound Recordings, Europas kulturelles und wissenschaftliches Erbe in einer digitalen Welt, Berlin, 21–22. Februar 2007, http://64.233.167.104/search?q=cache:USHGAPj0KAoJ:www.eudico.de/download/vortraege/schueller_%2520IASA_TC03_04_Berlin_02_07.pdf+IASA-TC+03&hl=en&ct=clnk&cd=2&gl=us&ie=UTF-8, accessed May 12, 2008.

12. Doug Boyd, "Preserving the Past," presentation at Oral History Preservation 101 Workshop, Kentucky Oral History Commission, Kentucky Historical Society, June 3, 2008:1–2.

13. Lossy codec reduction rates generally are at least 10:1 for audio and 300:1 for video, resulting in files that are greatly reduced in size. Lossy codecs are the standard for recording devices.

14. "TechEncyclopedia," http://www.techweb.com/encyclopedia/defineterm.jhtml?term=losslesscompression, accessed June 5, 2008.

15. Dietrich Schüller, *IASA-TC 03 und 04: Standards Related to the Long-Term Preservation and Digitisation of Sound Recordings,* 21–22. Februar 2007:26–33, http://64.233.167.104/search?q=cache:USHGAPj0KAoJ:www.eudico.de/download/vortraege/schueller_%2520IASA_TC03_04_Berlin_02_07.pdf+IASA-TC+03&hl=en&ct=clnk&cd=2&gl=us&ie=UTF-8, accessed May 12, 2008.

16. For more information, see "Videotaping Oral History" in Donald A. Ritchie, *Doing Oral History: A Practical Guide,* 2nd ed. (New York, NY: Oxford University Press, 2003): 134–154.

17. Stacy Ericson, revised by Troy Reeves, *A Field Notebook for Oral History,* 4th ed. (Boise, ID: Idaho Oral History Center, Idaho State Historical Society, 2001):29. Doug Boyd, correspondence to Barbara W. Sommer, September 22, 2008.

18. Doug Boyd, "Preserving the Past," June 3, 2008:4.

19. Doug Boyd, telephone conversation with Barbara W. Sommer, September 25, 2008.

20. Doug Boyd, "Gold CDs and Labels for CDs," H-Oralhist. http://h-net.msu.edu/cgi-bin/logbrowse, September 19, 2008, accessed September 19, 2008.

21. Doug Boyd, "Preserving the Past," June 3, 2008:4.

22. "TechEncyclopedia," http://www.techweb.com/encyclopedia/defineterm.jhtml?term=losslesscompression, accessed June 5, 2008.

23. Andy Kolovos, "Archival Quality CDs," H-Oralhist. http://h-net.msu.edu/cgi-bin/logbrowse, May 17, 2008, ac-cessed May 17, 2008. Dean Rehberger, "Archival Quality CDs," H-Oralhist. http://h-net.msu.edu/cgi-bin/logbrowse, May 17, 2008, accessed May 17, 2008. For further information, see the archives of the Association for Recorded Sound Collections (ARSC) at http://listserver.loc.gov/listarch/arsclist.html, accessed May 17, 2008.

24. Elizabeth Lowman, "Gold CDs and Labels for CDs," H-Oralhist. http://h-net.msu.edu/cgi-bin/logbrowse, September 13, 2008, accessed September 13, 2008. Andy Kolovos, "Gold CDs and Labels for CDs," H-Oralhist. http://h-net.msu.edu/cgi-bin/logbrowse, September 13, 2008, accessed September 13, 2008.

25. Doug Boyd, correspondence to Barbara W. Sommer, September 22, 2008. For more information, see Nancy MacKay, *Curating Oral Histories: From Interview to Archive* (Walnut Grove, CA: Left Coast Press, 2007):45.

26. Doug Boyd, "Gold CDs and Labels for CDs," H-Oralhist. http://h-net.msu.edu/cgi-bin/logbrowse, September 19, 2008, accessed September 19, 2008.

27. For more information about video file data storage, consult local or state archivists and the Oral History Association. Information about storage from Doug Boyd, telephone conversation with Barbara W. Sommer, September 25, 2008.

28. Susan Becker, "VideoTranscription Software," H-Oralhist. http://h-net.msu.edu/cgi-bin/logbrowse, May 17, 2008, accessed May 17, 2008. For more information see local or state archivists and the Oral History listserver.

29. Doug Boyd, telephone conversation with Barbara W. Sommer, June 16, 2008.

30. Bruce A. Bruemmer, "Access to Oral History: A National Agenda," *American Archivist* 54 (1991):494–501.

31. This is true for all analog recordings, including those made decades earlier. Original analog recordings, if they are the medium used to record the interview, are the archival masters, regardless of age. They should be maintained and cared for in the collections. Digitization is a process that puts analog recordings into a different format; it should never be used as a reason to discard archival masters. For up-to-date information on digitization procedures and standards, see Eric Weig, Kopana Terry, and Kathryn Lybarger, "Large-Scale Digitization of Oral History," *D-Lib Magazine* 13:5/6 (May/June 2007), http://www.dlib.org/dlib/may07/weig/05weig.html, accessed October 12, 2008.

CHAPTER 6

Interview Preparation

What is the best way to prepare for an oral history interview? Although the interview is the most-recognized part of the oral history process, a good interview requires thorough behind-the-scenes preparation. Interview preparation creates the structure on which the oral history is based. In Chapter Two, we provided an overview of the oral history planning process, including an outline of the interview preparation steps, but here we will discuss these steps in detail.

Interview preparation generally requires two steps: general project research and narrator-specific research. Often, people are attracted to an oral history project because they know about its subject and want to talk with people about it. Project coordinators need to direct this enthusiasm to the interview preparation process so that the interviews themselves will live up to everyone's expectations.

> Interview preparation involves general project research and individual narrator research.

Everyone involved in the project should participate in general project research regardless of how familiar some participants may be with the people, places, or themes to be explored. This joint research serves several purposes:

- It brings people together so they are all working from a common set of background materials toward a common goal.
- It makes participants aware of existing information and lays the groundwork for determining good oral history questions to fill in gaps in the historical record.
- It familiarizes interviewers with enough information about the subject to be able to keep the interview on track and spot the need for follow-up questions.

- It provides interviewers with details, such as names and dates, which can facilitate a good interview.

BEGIN BACKGROUND RESEARCH

The watchword on oral history projects is research. Research is essential for taking the project from the level of merely recording reminiscences to collecting the depth of information needed for good oral history. It is an important step even for those who are experts. Research helps define the project, provides background on topics to help explore them further, helps project leaders determine which topics are most important, suggests additional topics, and provides background information to inform the interviewer so he or she will be as prepared as possible for the interview.

Planners can help with this stage of project development by pulling together a basic information packet for all participants. This packet can include copies of written histories, newspaper articles, maps, photographs, drawings, excerpts from letters, diaries, and other primary-source materials. It can include as much information about the defined subject of the oral history project as planners deem necessary, but should not be overwhelming.

Widespread Internet access and powerful electronic tools for searching online databases are invaluable methods for quickly locating important and useful background information about nearly any topic imaginable. However, be aware of several potential electronic traps. First, unless the focus of your oral history project is fairly obscure or highly localized, searching the Internet for material related to your project can lead to informational quicksand that will mire you in an overwhelming mass of related material that no one could hope to sort through, much less understand. So cull through the pages of links and pull out only the material that pertains specifically to your project. Second, despite the appearance of providing a thorough search, Internet inquiries will provide access only to information that someone has decided to put online. Valuable private collections of primary-source materials—photographs, letters, personal papers and the like—may never be accessible electronically, but they could be pay dirt for planners seeking background information for an oral history project. How do you locate such treasures? Mainly by asking around—local libraries, community museums, area history buffs—and getting lucky. Likewise, if a quick Google search of your oral history topic leaves you empty-handed, don't assume no background information is available. County courthouses, corporate archives, schools, community civic clubs, and endless other types of organizations keep records—many of which never will be electronically accessible but which may be available to oral history project planners who ask politely to see them as part of the process of collecting background research.

With the packet of information as a base, project participants may wish to do additional research. This can include visits to the public library, historical society, newspaper archives, and specific places that have materials relevant to the project. Depending on the topics, this may involve research in local, state, or national facilities or more online research. Project advisory board members may help by finding collections to review and in identifying possible topics. The goal of all background research is to give project participants, especially the interviewers, a good base of knowledge to use in the interviews. If an interviewer is thoroughly prepared, the interview will be stronger. But because so much information can be available about some topics, planners will need to caution participants not to get bogged down at this stage by continually looking at yet one more source. Oral history interviewers need not become the world's living experts on topic X. Rather, they need to know enough about the topic to focus intelligently on the aspects of it that matter to their particular project.

Research for a project may be done by making notes with pencil and paper, notecards, or computers. In any case, it is always important to write down or enter any information that relates to the purpose of the oral history project. This includes names (with proper spellings), dates, facts, figures, and information (correct or incorrect) already on the record.[1] Interviewers will want to add to their basic packets any new information they find. All of this can help not only in defining interview topics, but in later development of specific questions.

It is always important to document clearly the source of the information. Keeping unclear notes often results in having to go back to clarify things—a waste of time. Many projects photocopy information if they can afford it, which can help with note taking. Photocopies, when properly identified and cited, are often a helpful addition to a project's collections. Even if projects have photocopy budgets to support research, project participants should photocopy only information that pertains specifically to the subject, rather than every item reviewed.

It is usually helpful to begin the research by looking into topics on the list. Which ones are already well documented? Is the documentation complete? Are there discrepancies among various sources of information? What is already on the record? Is it in need of further attention during an oral history interview? What information is missing or inaccurate and should be covered in an oral history interview? What topics are not documented well at all? How important is it to document them? What questions should be asked about a topic? What subtopics come to light that help define each topic further? What questions need to be asked about a subtopic?

Research will probably bring up new topics as well. As new topics come to light, they can be added to the list and the same questions applied to them. Reviewing the research that is collected will help project leaders determine what should be covered in the interviews and why this information should be collected.

COMPILE A BIBLIOGRAPHY

Project participants should keep a list of all information sources they use. This will be compiled as the project bibliography. It becomes an end product of the oral history project, serves as a reference tool for newcomers to the project and as a source for future researchers who want to know what background information created the foundation for the interviews.

DEVELOP A LIST OF DATES AND EVENTS

Working with the background information, one person or a small group should develop a timeline, identifying milestones important to the topic. Not only will this encourage everyone to focus on the materials, it will also result in a useful resource document that helps guide continuing research. When you're ready to begin the interviews, it also serves as a good interviewing tool.

MAKE A LIST OF THEMES OR TOPICS TO INCLUDE IN THE INTERVIEW

In addition to giving project participants information about the subject, general background research helps

Sample List of Names and Dates

1901   Brothers Martin and Marvin Jones develop a product for preventing power loss in engines. The Jones brothers were awarded a patent on their invention.

1902   The Jones Production Company was incorporated with an issue of 100,000 shares of capital stock at $.75/share.

1909   Everett Smith joined the company as general operations manager. He developed the major market for the product.

1914   The company became known as Jones Company, Inc.

1918   The company received its first government contract.

1921   The company employed 350 people prior to the "farm crash" and the start of the agricultural depression.

1927   The company began to diversify its product line by adding smaller sizes in an attempt to stave off losses.

1934   The company was sold to Charles Anderson and Sons.

1939   The company began making engines that featured its product.

1940   The company received a government contract to make engines using its product. It employed 750 people working three shifts.

1944   The company received an award for its war work.

1945   The plant voted to unionize under the leadership of John Ross.

1949   Charles Anderson retired and his sons, John and George, took over company management.

1950   The company built a new plant at 37th and Randolph Streets. The old plant at 12th and Elm Streets was torn down and the land was sold to the city. Employment was at 450 people working two shifts.

1953   The company received a government contract to build engines.

1956   The company negotiated a deal with Montgomery Ward to distribute engines through their stores.

1959   The union staged a major strike for better wages and conditions. The strike lasted for 3 months and resulted in raises up to $3.00 per hour and increased safety procedures.

1962   The plant burned to the ground.

1964   The plant was re-built and had its grand opening. The product line was expanded to include engine-related products. Employment was at 300.

1968   The workforce was fully integrated for the first time.

1973   The Anderson brothers sold the company to a XYZ Company, Inc., a national distributor of engines and related equipment.

1979   Sales were affected by the Energy Crisis. Employment at 200.

1985   XYZ Company expanded the product line to include engine-related equipment from plants it owned in other states.

1991   XYZ Company sold the company to Engines International, Ltd., a London-based manufacturing company.

1998   Engines International, Ltd. sold its holdings, including the company, to Sheridan, Inc., an international conglomerate.

2002   The company celebrated its centennial. Employment at 375.

Figure 6.1.   A sample list of dates and events for an oral history project.

planners identify topics or areas where information is sketchy or ambiguous or reveals mysterious, unanswered questions. These are all topics you'll want to cover in the oral history interviews. Oral history is used to document information—including opinions, interpretations, and points of view—that otherwise is unavailable and subject to loss. By familiarizing themselves with existing information, interviewers can identify gaps in what is already available and determine how to fill them through oral history.

> Developing a list of themes or topics is a first step in focusing the interview.

Background researchers should keep a list of topics either omitted or inadequately covered in the written materials and any other topic ideas to include in an interview. Coordinators should regularly look over these lists, analyzing how each topic relates to the mission statement. All ideas that meet the criteria should be included on a master interview topic list. Review and analyze these lists regularly to keep the project focused. They will become the basis for designing the oral history interviews.

IDENTIFY POTENTIAL NARRATORS AND DETERMINE THEMES OR TOPICS TO COVER WITH EACH OF THEM

General project research is an essential way to identify potential narrators. Although you might know from the outset some of the people you'll want to interview, general background research often leads to others whose knowledge is essential to project success. Background research will also help identify additional, perhaps previously unknown, types of information needed to fill gaps in knowledge, leading project coordinators to seek out potential narrators who can fill those gaps. The background research also can help you decide which people might have enough information for several interview sessions, while others might require only a shorter, single interview session.

As a rule of thumb, be conservative in planning the number of interviews you can complete. If your initial goal is to interview everyone whose name surfaces, the task will be so daunting that everyone involved will be frustrated and defeated from the start. Instead, begin with no more than three to five interviews—up to 10 hours. Set a goal of ensuring these are well researched, well structured, and fully processed. When this is

done, look realistically at what it took to meet this goal and determine what is manageable for your group to complete additional interviews. A handful of well-done interviews can inspire confidence in the project and energize participants to keep going. Having something concrete to show for your efforts also can generate more financial support for future work.

Oral history focuses on collecting firsthand knowledge. As such, narrators should be selected because of their knowledge about the interview themes and topics. They also should represent a variety of perspectives and backgrounds. In fact, an oral history project often specifically intends to seek out perspectives that are not already on the record. This will enhance the results of your oral history project, broadening the base of information you collect.

A project Edward Nelson and Robert "Skip" Drake and others developed several years ago in Minnesota to collect information about the Civilian Conservation Corps (CCC), for example, easily could have used all of its available resources interviewing the men who enrolled in the camps. The network was still strong, relatively little documentation was on the written record about enrollees' time in the CCC camps, and narrators could be found quickly because many were willing to tell their stories. But they could only tell one part of the story. This oral history project included others, such as: U.S. Army personnel who ran the work camps in which the enrollees lived; representatives from the agencies that developed the projects on which enrollees worked, including former forest service personnel and U.S. Army personnel, and others involved with various projects or agencies; adult work leaders and crew leaders assigned to supervise enrollees at work; and members of racial or ethnic groups who were or were not welcomed into the camps. Making an effort to include all sides of the issues enhances the project and gives it the depth that characterizes good oral history.

Lists of possible narrators are sometimes easily compiled. At other times, it can take considerable legwork to find people who have firsthand knowledge about the project's themes or topics and who are good prospective narrators. In addition to relying on project research to uncover names of possible narrators, advisory board members and informal networks of individuals knowledgeable about the project and its purpose can add to the list. Depending on the subject, informal networks can generate a long list of possible narrators that will have to be winnowed down to a manageable size.

Good narrators for an oral history interview are people who:

- have firsthand, previously undocumented information about project topics or themes
- represent all sides of an issue
- have strong powers of observation
- have a good memory
- can communicate effectively
- have an ability to understand the basics of the oral history process as explained by the interviewer or project coordinator and are willing to participate, including signing a donor form
- are willing to give an account of their memories of the project topics or themes
- are reasonably comfortable with interview equipment in either audio or video settings.

Narrators inevitably bring their own biases to project topics or themes. Their memories also reflect their perspectives on what happened, the ways in which they have organized their understanding of the past, and their frames of reference on what is or is not important. They are also often influenced by thoughts and ideas that have occurred since the event or time period. Narrators are chosen for a project because their views about it are important. Each narrator brings a unique perspective to the project's topics or themes; collectively, those perspectives enrich the historical record.

It often helps to think about choosing possible narrators in terms of the information each can bring to your project. Narrators may be chosen for knowledge about a certain time period or because they represent a certain perspective about an event related to the themes or topics. They may be chosen because they have a long-term perspective, although, while you will want to take age and health factors into consideration, it is never necessary to interview the oldest person around just because he or she is old. They may be chosen because of their knowledge about the themes or topics. It is also not always necessary to interview the most visible local historian or the most famous person associated with an event. Often, in fact, such local notables have either told or written their story many times and it is already a part of the existing record. Sometimes they have repeated the stories so often, almost as a rehearsed performance, that it's impossible for them to explore the event more deeply, a hallmark of good oral history. Project coordinators should instead look for people who have firsthand knowledge and are willing to communicate this information

clearly and effectively, answering the interviewer's questions to the best of their ability. Often, they may be people who have information about just one theme or one aspect of the project but whose perspective is nonetheless central to fully exploring the topic.

The names of potential narrators should go into a pool for consideration. Depending on your project's resources, choices will have to be made. The most helpful approach is to set priorities, identifying narrators whom you think are most critical to include and working down the list as resources are available. Although you may identify additional criteria based on the needs of a project, a person's ability to provide information about the interview topics should be the primary factor when choosing narrators. Using this as a guide to match potential narrators to interview topics about which they are most knowledgeable will help organize the project and will ensure inclusion of narrators whose information is most useful.

Project participants, including the coordinators, should decide who will be interviewed. Although supporters and others interested in the project will have ideas about potential narrators, project coordinators and interviewers who have been involved in the research are in the best position to know who should be interviewed and what the interview priorities should be. Names of potential narrators will continue to surface as the project progresses, and the narrator list and priorities could change based on this new information. As mentioned previously, it is not a good idea to advertise for narrators. You should reserve the right to determine who will be on the final narrator list. A public solicitation for narrators often carries with it the implied promise of an interview, which may hamper the project's final results.

Once possible narrators have been identified, project coordinators should begin contacting them, requesting their involvement in the project. This is usually done with a letter explaining the project and providing background about their expected involvement. A sample letter, along with samples of other suggested correspondence, is included in Appendix A. The designated interviewer should follow up the letter with a telephone call. This provides an opportunity for the interviewer and narrator to talk informally, allows the interviewer to answer additional questions, and gives the narrator a chance to make a verbal commitment to be interviewed. Some narrators, when first contacted, may be unsure of their ability to contribute effectively to the project. The telephone call can allow the interviewer to address these questions and concerns.

After the first narrators have agreed to be a part of the project, interviewers should begin narrator-specific research. This step creates the structure for the interview. An interviewer should work on only one interview at a time, selecting or being assigned narrators in priority order from the pool of names.

> Narrator-specific research helps structure an interview.

Narrator-specific research involves learning as much as possible about the person to be interviewed and his or her role in the subject at hand. This may include such details as work history, personal history, family history, political history—anything that gives the interviewer the necessary background to ask good project-related questions with appropriate follow-up. Such research also helps build rapport between interviewer and narrator during the interview. The interviewer should rely on as wide a variety of background materials as necessary to become fully informed. This often includes online research as well as a review of related interviews and trips to the historical society, library, newspaper office, and other sites containing resource information. It may also include review of maps, visits to sites that are important to the interview, and additional work with primary sources. As with the general background research, it is important not to become bogged down in the wealth of information that might be available about some narrators. In other cases, it might be difficult to find documented information about a specific narrator. Asking the person to provide biographical information prior to the interview, such as that listed in the biographical information form, can help by making additional information available to guide the research. In any case, narrator-specific research can focus on the context of the narrator's background to give the interviewer as much knowledge as possible.

DEVELOP AN INTERVIEW OUTLINE OR GUIDE
Using the master topic list as a guide and combining it with information obtained in the narrator-specific research, the interviewer develops the interview outline or guide. This is not a scripted list of questions. It is a list of topics to cover in the interview, often combined with background notes the interviewer will find helpful in eliciting information in the most professional way possible. Project coordinators should review the interviewer's guide to make sure topics covered are consistent with the project's goals.

After defining the interview focus, the interviewer should think about narrator-specific topics that can help structure the interview. These can be organized on the interview outline by sequence of events. It is helpful to list the topics in the order the narrator may want to discuss them. Many interviewers find that approaching topics chronologically is helpful, since that is often how people think. If the questions are likely to include emotionally charged or sensitive topics, it's usually best to plan for those later in the interview, after the interviewer has had a chance to establish rapport with the narrator. The interviewer should use the outline to guide the interview, but should be prepared to follow the narrator's train of thought and remain flexible in how and when topics are introduced.

> The interview outline is the list of topics and notes about questions specific to the narrator's knowledge. The interviewer uses the outline to guide the interview.

Within each subject area, the interviewer should list on the interview outline the points to be covered and background information about each. This will help identify the specifics to be discussed during the interview while providing the interviewer with details about existing information. The outline should be organized so the interview will flow smoothly from one topic to another while allowing for the inclusion of information that may be unexpected and yet relevant to the project.

The interview outline should reflect the purpose of the project. For example, if the focus of an interview is on a person's experiences as a nurse in the Korean War, the interviewer probably would not take interview time to ask detailed, in-depth questions about union involvement or farming activities, though the person may have much information on those subjects, too. Similarly, any pre-interview contacts or correspondence with the narrator should make clear that the Korean War nursing experiences will be the focus of the interview. Based on what is already known about the designated subject of an oral history project, the interviewer will want to concentrate on eliciting information the narrator can add that fits overall project goals.

The interview outline should contain as much information as the interviewer needs for the interview.

BIOGRAPHICAL INFORMATION FORM

Name _Jane Doe_

Address (home) _456 Smith Lane_

Amarillo, Texas

Address (work) _24679 Post Road_

Amarillo, Texas

Telephone (home) _412-724-9675_ (work) _412-723-1234_ E-mail _jd@adr.net_

Birth Date and Year _9/27/42_

Birth Place _Houston, Texas_

Occupation _teacher_

Spouse or Closest Living Relative _John Doe_

Maiden Name (if applicable) _Smith_

Biographical Information (include information applicable to the interview):

John & Joan Smith – parents
James & Janie Doe – children
B.A. in English 1963
M.A. in Education 1967

Form Filled Out By _J. D._
Date _10/29/07_

Figure 6.2.   An Example of a filled-out Biographical Information Form.

This can include research notes about names, places, dates, or any other details that will help jog the narrator's memory. It should not be so voluminous, however, that the interviewer spends more time shuffling notes and looking for details than asking questions and listening to the answers.

As seen in figure 6.3, the interview outline should not be written in question format and doesn't need to be in complete sentences. An oral history interview is not a scripted telemarketing survey. Listing discussion topics rather than questions encourages an easy flow of information between interviewer and narrator and helps keep the interviewer's focus on the narrator and his or her responses rather than on reading one question after another. The interviewer will want to use the information in the interview outline to frame questions, to offer specifics that help the narrator place a question in context, and to develop follow-up questions.

Interviewers should be familiar with everything in the interview guide and should know the reasons for including each topic and how each fits into the overall project structure. They should be prepared to hear new, firsthand information and to clarify anything they don't immediately understand. They should also be prepared to be flexible, since a narrator might want to talk about things in a different order than listed on the interview outline. The interviewer should use the outline to ensure all topics have been fully covered. Finally, interviewers should never include opinions about what they think, either on the interview outline or during the interview. Interviewers should approach the interview as impartial, nonjudgmental facilitators who are prepared to pin down information, ask pointed questions, and probe beneath the surface for new information about the interview topics.

SCHEDULE THE INTERVIEW
When nearing completion of the narrator-specific research and development of the interview outline, the interviewer should contact the narrator to schedule the interview. This may be done by telephone, but should be followed up with a letter confirming date, time, and location. The letter should also include a request for a photograph of the narrator for the master file.

Oral history projects usually include a face-to-face pre-interview or a preliminary telephone contact with potential narrators at this point. This involves a short, general discussion with the person about the interview and gives the interviewer a chance to introduce himself or herself to the narrator, which helps build rap-

port. Some interviewers like to collect biographical information from the narrator at this point. It also provides an opportunity to answer any further questions about the oral history project and to explain the recording process and the use of the donor form. And it can be a good time to discuss the interview topics in general terms with the narrator, though there are several words of caution here. Be careful not to give the narrator lists of the questions to be asked. You may think this will help the narrator prepare for the interview, but in reality it often results only in rehearsed answers, not the vibrant responses with the depth that oral history at its best can elicit. Occasionally, narrators who have seen a complete list of questions will write out their answers, which they then will want to read into the microphone. This is not oral history. Sharing the interview outline also can inhibit inclusion of any additional information not on the outline, information that may add depth to the interview. And do not allow the pre-interview discussion to include the telling of specific information you want to cover in the interview. When this happens and you then ask for the information in the interview, the narrator often either refers to the earlier conversation rather than answering the question or repeats the story in a less lively way than you heard it initially. As a follow-up, the interview confirmation letter can summarize your discussion, listing the general topics to be covered in the interview.

CHOOSE THE SETUP FOR THE INTERVIEW
A face-to-face pre-interview meeting also can serve another important purpose: It allows the interviewer to check out the setting where the interview will take place. Many oral history interviews occur in the narrator's home, a familiar environment that can have a positive effect on the interview. Schools, museums, places of business, libraries, even recording studios are other common interview locations, and each has its own advantages and disadvantages. The goal is to conduct oral history interviews in places where you can control sound (and visual) quality and where the narrator and interviewer will not be interrupted. Business offices, for example, are appropriate places for interviews only if the narrator can prevent telephone interruptions. Whatever the setting, it should be a place where the narrator will be comfortable and where the setting itself does not create distractions or make the narrator ill at ease. (See the checklists below for details about the mechanics of setting up an oral history interview.)

Narrator Name
Project Name
Place and Date of Interview
Interviewer Name

The narrator, John Doe, is a former president of the foundation.

Narrator Background
 Your background and education
 How hear about foundation
 What interested you about foundation, why become involved
  Recruited, accepted position on board
 Foundation mission and purpose as described to you
 Describe board training/orientation
 On board from 1975–2003—time of transition and change
Narrator Board Involvement
 First vice chair (dates)
  Served under presidents (names)
  Major board initiatives during your tenure as first vice chair
Your goals as first vice chair, discuss
 Treasurer (dates)
  Served under presidents (names)
  Describe major initiatives or changes during your tenure
 Audit Committee and chair (dates)
  Served under presidents (names)
  Roles and responsibilities
 Governance Committee (dates)
  Served under presidents (names)
  Describe major initiatives or changes during your tenure
 Investment committee (dates)
  Served under presidents (names)
  Describe major initiatives or changes during your tenure
 Grants committee and chair (dates)
  Chair (dates)
  Served under presidents (names)
  Major grants initiatives of foundation during your tenure
   (Insert names of each)
  Discuss priorities and how determine
   Changes in priorities, describe
  Mission of foundation and how carried out
  Roles and responsibilities of committee and board members

(Continue with questions about narrator's work as longtime foundation board member)

Figure 6.3. Sample of Interview Outline, also called Interview Guide

Thinking through the setting is an important part of the process, for it can affect the outcome of the interview. As an example, one community embarked on a project documenting the installation of missiles in its vicinity during the height of the Cold War. Because project planners were interested in creating both audio and video recordings, they decided to do most of the interviews in a public studio or an adjoining room in the city library. The same topics and themes were covered in all the interviews, and the choices about who was to be interviewed in which setting were based primarily on the availability of the narrators. One person specifically did not want to be interviewed on camera at the library and another narrator would agree only to an audio interview at home. While the setting of an interview alone is unlikely to be the sole factor contributing to particular narrator behavior or responses, the project leaders noted some curious differences in interview content that seemed to be related to the interview setting. The video interviews in the studio at the public library featured repeated tellings of the more dominant public side of the story expressing support for the missile installations. Interviews in the adjoining room, in which there was no video and only the interviewer and narrator were present, produced a less commonly voiced private side of the story, including expressions of fears for the future. And the narrator who insisted on being interviewed at home recalled active resistance to the missile installation, reflecting what had been a decidedly minority viewpoint in the community and one that even many years after the fact was not widely acknowledged in public.

Did the more public, formal setting, complete with interviewer and camera operator, lend itself to eliciting the popular public narrative about the missile installation? Did a non-threatening home environment with only an interviewer present create a safety zone for the narrator to express an unpopular view? One can never be certain. But the narrators' responses at least suggest that the context in which an interview takes place—including the presence or absence of video—is an important element affecting an interview's content and character.

PRACTICE WITH THE RECORDING EQUIPMENT
Interviewers should be thoroughly trained on using the recording equipment and should practice with it repeatedly before using it for the first time in an interview. They should know how to use it unobtrusively and with confidence and how to handle minor diffi-

culties in the field. Always begin by reading the manual that comes with the equipment. It will help you understand what all the dials, switches, and buttons mean and how each works to control the recording process. You will want to know how to set sound levels and how to troubleshoot.

> Always remember to practice using the recorder before the interview.

Remember that the microphone is a critical part of the recording process and has capabilities and limitations with which the interviewer needs to be familiar. (See the discussion in Chapter Five about types of microphones for oral history interviews.) Some researchers who do other kinds of field recordings focus the microphone primarily on the narrator with less emphasis on hearing the interviewer's questions. But in an oral history interview, the exchanges between the interviewer and narrator are critical to understanding the information that emerges. So it is important to record both speakers, documenting clearly what questions were asked and in what order. This helps future users understand the context of the interview and, thus, the information in it.

HEAD OUT FOR THE INTERVIEW
You're almost ready now for the next big step: conducting the oral history interview. All the planning so far is aimed at making the process flow as smoothly as possible. Some oral history projects put interview kits together that include all the necessary tools. Such a kit can include:

- recorder
- microphone, cables, and microphone stand
- AC adapter/transformer and extension cord
- media (it is wise to take more than you could possibly need)
- batteries
- notebook (often in "steno" format, six by nine inches)
- pencils
- folder containing the donor form (two copies— one for the master file and one to leave with the narrator), the interview outline, the biographical information form, and copies of the letters to the narrator

- camera to take a picture of the narrator in interview setting (this is necessary for audio interviews and is helpful to add to the master file for video interviews).

Finally, arrive on time. A prompt arrival will start the process out right. If there has not been a pre-interview meeting, this may be the first time the interviewer and narrator meet, in which case it is even more important not to be late.

Preparation for the interview is not glamorous. Nor is it as exciting as the actual interview. Without adequate preparation, however, the oral history interview will not fulfill its potential.

CHECKLIST FOR SETTING UP AN AUDIO INTERVIEW

☐ The narrator is in a comfortable spot where he or she can relax and focus on the interview and where the narrator and interviewer will not be interrupted.

☐ Pay special attention to the audible environment. Be sure that the narrator's chair doesn't squeak or make other noises and that other audible distractions—pets that bark, meow, or chirp, chiming clocks, dishwashers, telephones, lawn mowers, and the like—are minimized. People will tune out such extraneous noises but recorders will faithfully record them all. Ask the narrator to turn off any cell phones, and be sure to turn yours off, too.

☐ The interviewer should sit no more than about six feet away, facing the narrator. The two should be able to hear each other clearly and maintain eye contact.

☐ Use a table or other sturdy surface next to the interviewer to hold the recorder within easy reach to monitor it and change media as necessary. It is best to position the recorder out of the narrator's direct line of vision so he or she will focus on the interviewer, not the equipment, but *never* hide it from view. Oral historians do not engage in clandestine recording.

☐ An omnidirectional microphone should be placed no more than two or three feet from and pointed at the narrator. Carry a long enough microphone cable to facilitate the best placement of the microphone and recorder.

☐ If lavaliere microphones are used, clip one on the interviewer and one on the narrator, each about 10 inches from the speaker's mouth. Remove jewelry, scarves or jackets made of crisp fabric. All can cause rustling noises as the speakers move. (For more details about microphone choices, see Chapter Five.)

☐ Plug the audio recorder into a wall or floor outlet whenever possible, bringing long extension cords to facilitate this. Be sure to place extension cords in such a way that no one will trip on them.

☐ Carry backup batteries for the recorder to use in emergencies or where electrical outlets are unavailable or impractical to use.

☐ Decline offers of food or drink. While interviewers will want to be sociable, an oral history interview is not, strictly speaking, a social occasion. Coffee cups on saucers, ice in glasses, pop tops on cans being opened, and other food or drink consumption all make noise the recorder will pick up. Narrators will understand if you explain to them that you want to minimize any extraneous noise that might mar the sound quality of the recorded interview.

☐ Do a sound check with the equipment to be sure it is working properly and the voices are being picked up clearly. Keep it simple by asking the narrator to give his or her name and address and chatting about something neutral while unobtrusively checking recording levels. Fussing over the equipment can make an interviewer nervous.

☐ Use headphones to continuously monitor the sound, allowing you to identify and correct any problems.

CHECKLIST FOR SETTING UP A VIDEO INTERVIEW

☐ Read the checklist for setting up an audio interview. Many of the considerations for arranging the interview setting are the same for both formats.

☐ Refer to the section of Chapter Five that discusses the questions to consider in determining how or whether video recording will enhance the oral history.

☐ It is seldom advisable for the interviewer also to be the equipment operator in a video interview, unless the interviewer is both a skilled oral historian and a skilled camera operator.

☐ Unless a video interview will take place in a studio or other controlled setting, plan to visit the site in advance, preferably with people who will be operating the camera, microphones, lights, or any other equipment that will be needed for the recording session.

☐ Because a video interview likely will involve more staff, who generally may be paid, and possibly rented locations such as production studios, consider developing a more detailed interview outline to assure the best use of a specific block of time.

You may not be able to extend the interview even if the narrator has important things still to say, so try to make sure the interview covers all the essentials in the allotted time.

☐ Indoor video interviews should be shot in soft light that appropriately illuminates the setting. Avoid overhead lighting, which results in poor quality video. Also avoid fluorescent lighting, which gives a blue tint to the video. The narrator should not sit in front of a window or other source of natural light.

☐ The background setting should not overwhelm the narrator. A plain neutral or blue backdrop is a good choice, if available. In any event, check that items in the background do not appear to be sprouting out of the narrator's head.

☐ Always frame the shot so it is in focus with the narrator centered in the picture and at eye level with the camera, a psychologically and emotionally neutral position. Give the narrator what videographers call "head room" and "look space," meaning the camera is not at too close range.

☐ A head shot from the mid-chest or shoulders is customary; never cut the person visually at the neck, waist, or knees.

☐ If more than one narrator is in the video interview, position everyone so all their faces are clearly visible and so that the interviewer can maintain eye contact with all of them. This is sometimes done using a V format, with the interviewer sitting on the open end facing the narrators.

☐ Narrators should be asked to wear uncluttered clothing in neutral or dark colors. White shirts and blouses reflect light and make filming natural skin tones difficult.

☐ The camera should be placed on a tripod to assure stability and focused on the narrator with little or no change in the camera beyond the essentials to capture movement once the shot has been framed.

☐ Even though the camera has a zoom lens, do not zoom in and out on the narrator. This is a televised interview technique that oral historians do not use. Instead, use the zoom lens for close-ups of photo-graphs or other materials you wish to document as part of the interview.

☐ The interviewer's questions should be heard clearly, but an interviewer generally is not seen, unless the interview is being conducted in sign language. The interviewer should be positioned to look directly at the narrator, with the camera over the interviewer's shoulder. If project coordinators want the interviewer to be seen, a second camera will be needed because one camera always should be on the narrator.

☐ When filming on location, be aware that lighting and background sound elements can change during the video recording, so plan for such possibilities. Always stop the interview if noise from airplanes, highways, farm machinery, or other intrusive sounds occur and wait for conditions to return to normal.

☐ Record video interviews simultaneously on audio equipment to be used for transcribing and as an archival backup of the interview.

☐ Project planners usually choose to video record interviews because the physical environment illustrates important interview information, so be sure to video record the setting, including specific items or places, before or after the interview.

☐ Still photographs or three-dimensional objects that are to be documented as part of the video process should be propped up on a stand against a black background.

Remember that video interviews, just like their audio counterparts, are primary-source materials; they will not look like a scripted, produced documentary. Audio and video interview excerpts often are used effectively in documentaries and other productions, but the interviews themselves should be kept intact and handled as primary-source material.

NOTE

1. David Kyvig and Myron Marty include several chapters of helpful, common-sense research guidelines in their book, *Nearby History: Exploring the Past around You*, 2nd ed. (Walnut Creek, CA: AltaMira Press, 2000).

CHAPTER 7

The Interview

What interviewing techniques lend themselves to creating good oral histories? The interview is the most visible part of the oral history project. Good interviewing techniques are integral to its success. In this chapter we suggest a model for conducting an oral history interview. We will then review additional techniques interviewers find useful and discuss special interviewing circumstances.

GETTING THE INTERVIEW UNDERWAY

After you have organized the interview setting, you will want to ask the narrator if he or she has any questions before the interview begins.

The Interview

Remember to keep the interview setting as comfortable as possible. This will help the narrator concentrate on the interview.

It is important to establish rapport with the narrator. A sense of trust between narrator and interviewer helps make a good interview.

Listen (and look) carefully for noise sources, such as ringing phones and chiming clocks, that will undermine the sound quality of the interview.

Take a little time with the narrator before beginning the interview to talk and relax.

Always be on time for an interview.

This is a good time to review the language in the donor form and to let the narrator know he or she will be asked to sign it as soon as the interview is over. Some interviewers also take this time to ask the narrator to fill out a biographical information form to keep a record of the person's name, address, and other particulars. (A sample biographical information form is in Appendix A.) After an equipment sound check, the interviewer will want to begin with a recorded introduction, such as:

The following interview was conducted with _____ (name of narrator) on behalf of the _____ for the _____ Oral History Project. It took place on _____ (date) at _____ (place). The interviewer is _____ (name).

Additional descriptive information may be given, but is not necessary. The introduction should be brief, to the point, and thorough. Adding too much information about the expected interview topics could give the impression that the interviewer is not interested in information on other topics that, when brought up, could lead to interesting, important, new, and pertinent information. A similar introduction should begin each subsequent recording media used for the interview to avoid orphaned recordings whose identifying features are lost.

The interviewer should always record an introduction before starting the interview. It should include:

- name of narrator
- name of interviewer
- place of interview
- date of interview
- name of oral history project
- name of repository
- media or track number

This is usually done in the interview setting and is a signal to the narrator that the interview is ready to begin.

As a rule of thumb, the interview should unfold in chronological order and generally should be structured to elicit facts about the time, place, or event that is the focus of the interview as well as the narrator's thoughts about and analysis of the facts. Even if an interview focuses on a specific subject or event, the interviewer should begin with questions about personal background. This should be brief, but is a good way to start virtually every interview because the questions are easy for the narrator to answer, and it provides a context for evaluating subsequent information the narrator gives. Some interviewers have found that initial questions about a narrator's work experience prove useful in getting a reticent narrator to relax, open up, and talk freely about past experiences.

After these background questions, move to the interview topics, beginning with when, how, and why the narrator initially became involved with the subject or event. This sets the stage for the narrator to tell the story from the beginning. Then move to questions about the subject or event. Prompted by open-ended questions, the narrator will talk about what happened, what he or she did or observed, and what others did. After listening to the narrator's account, a thoroughly prepared interviewer will be able to explore the information further and attempt to clarify any apparent contradictions with other written or spoken accounts. Exploring contradictions, not resolving them, is the point of the interview: our understanding of the past can be enriched by looking at events or actions from different perspectives. Narrators also will sometimes contradict themselves, and if they do, interviewers should strive for clarification by gently calling attention to the apparent contradictions. Sometimes it will turn out that a narrator simply misspoke. But in other cases, a narrator's response can offer fascinating insights into how the person tries to reconstruct and make sense of the past—one of the multiple layers of meaning that can be embedded in an oral history interview.

Finally, ask the narrator to assess the experience or event. Why did things happen as they did? What did the narrator think about it then? What does he or she think about it now? Asking for the narrator's analysis and reflections obtains insight into his or her thinking, another important aspect of oral history. Pragmatically, it also signals that the interview is winding down and provides for a graceful closing.[1]

Interviewers working with one person on a series of life interviews will follow the same process of beginning with questions that are easy for the narrator to answer, then moving to the subject of the interview, and finally assessing the information as the interview winds down. Life interviews are often organized around specific periods in the person's life. This gives each interview session a focus for both interviewer and narrator.

Oral history interviews generally last from one and a half to two hours. An interview of three hours or longer often ends with extreme narrator and interviewer fatigue. If you think you'll need extensive information from one narrator, plan for more than one interview session. Keep track of the time during an interview, making sure not to tire out the narrator before covering key points. Judging how much time to spend on personal questions at the beginning and on questions that set up the body of the interview is the interviewer's responsibility and should be carefully considered and thoughtfully addressed.

Use open-ended questions: "Tell me about …" "Describe …"

Don't be judgmental or let your own opinions show. The interview is the narrator's time to tell his or her story.

Use your background research to prompt the narrator as necessary. Reminders of names, dates, places, and events are helpful.

Ask about thoughts and feelings. It is the subjective information that helps make oral history such an interesting primary source.

Don't interrupt the narrator. Wait until he or she is finished to ask another question.

Be prepared to ask follow-up questions to clarify information.

Don't argue with the narrator's information. If you question its accuracy, politely ask the narrator for greater elaboration. You may find the narrator's story actually sets the written record straight.

Be thoroughly familiar with the research and the topics you intend to pursue. It breaks the rhythm of the interview to be constantly referring to the interview outline or to other notes.

Know how to operate the recording equipment. Practice repeatedly before the interview and always do a sound check before beginning.

Thank the narrator when finished. Follow this with a written thank-you letter.

INTERVIEW GUIDELINES AND TECHNIQUES

Always keep the ethics of the situation in mind. An oral history interview is not a casual two-way conversation, a social call, or a heated debate over the interpretation of the past. Narrators are entitled to respect for their stories.

Rely on open-ended questions. They elicit the most information. Examples are: "What were you told?" "How did you celebrate Christmas?" "Tell me about . . ." "Describe . . ." The importance of asking open-ended questions cannot be overemphasized. As Donald A. Ritchie pointed out in his book *Doing Oral History*, open-ended questions allow narrators "to volunteer their own accounts, to speculate on matters, and to have enough time to include all the material they think relevant to the subject." He added that open-ended questions also empower narrators, shifting the balance of power from the interviewer to the narrator. Through this, the narrator can shape the "course of the interview rather than responding passively."[2]

Use neutral, not leading, questions. Asking the narrator "Why don't you like living here?" will not result in as complete an answer as the more neutral question "Tell me about living here." Questions beginning with *how, what, when, why, where,* and *who* are often used to introduce a subject or to follow up an initial statement. They can help clarify an answer and can elicit further information. Some scholars have noted that within every question is hidden a clue to its answer, something oral historians need to keep in mind as they frame questions.[3] An interviewer, for example, might be tempted to think that "How do you like living here?" is a more neutral version of "Why don't you like living here?" It's certainly less inflammatory, but still not as neutral as "Tell me about living here."

Ask only one question at a time, not a smorgasbord of questions that will puzzle the narrator. If clarification is needed, make sure your elaboration does not lead the narrator to believe you expect a particular type of answer.

Avoid the temptation to share your personal agreements or disagreements with the narrator's views. Your opinions on the subject are not the focus of the interview. Some narrators, believing the purpose of the interview is an equal exchange of views like that encountered at a roundtable discussion or cocktail party, will try to draw an interviewer's opinions into the exchange. If that happens, an interviewer might satisfy the narrator's curiosity by one of several neutral responses like: "I never thought of it that way." Or "That's very interesting." Or "I can see your point." But it may occasionally be necessary for the interviewer simply to explain forthrightly that the purpose of an oral history interview is to document the narrator's views, not the interviewer's.

Keep your focus on the narrator. Don't show off your knowledge. Your background research is intended to help you draw out the narrator, but bragging about what you know is likely to have the opposite effect.

Listen carefully without interrupting the narrator. The goal in an oral history interview is to collect in-depth answers by posing focused, clearly stated, open-ended, neutral questions.

If the narrator insists on telling a rehearsed story, listen politely and let him or her finish. Then go back and ask additional questions that will get the narrator to go beyond the rehearsed performance.

Concentrate on what the narrator is saying. Take notes and wait until he or she has finished speaking. Then ask follow-up questions for clarification or to develop new information that did not emerge in the research process.

Watch for hints, such as pauses or slight changes in voice, that indicate the narrator may have additional thoughts or feelings to describe and ask respectful follow-up questions. Sometimes narrators may indicate their feelings about subjects being discussed through body language. These are nonverbal responses to questions, such as pointing a finger, leaning toward the interviewer, leaning away from the interviewer, crossing the arms and legs, shifting or moving noticeably, breaking eye contact, and talking slower or faster than normal. You will want to be aware of these clues and respond to them as necessary. It is sometimes helpful to respectfully mention a nonverbal response and ask the narrator to discuss his or her feelings in more depth.

Use information identified through background and narrator-specific research to help facilitate a smooth interview. This may be as simple as supplying the correct date for an event or the name of someone connected with the event. Providing such information saves the narrator the frustration of trying to remember specifics or the possible embarrassment of giving incorrect information. It also indicates the project is important enough to have interviewers who are thoroughly prepared.

It helps to ask the narrator to put an event or memory into the context of time and place as much as possible. This may be done by encouraging the narrator to think in terms of people and places that have ties to the interview topics. For example, one narrator, when asked to think about a specific subject in this way, closed his eyes and asked the interviewer what year he should put himself back to. This helped him put the memory into context. Another technique is to ask the narrator to describe what a place or event from the past looked like. For people with keen visual memories, this can be an important memory-jogging technique. Use the list of names and dates as necessary to help the narrator put events in context.

Photographs, maps, drawings, and three-dimensional objects are useful aids, although careful verbal descriptions of each will have to be given in audio interviews. The interviewer might say, for example: "So Great-Uncle Joe is the second from the left wearing a bowler hat." In a video recorded interview, if a narrator has photographs or other objects pertinent to the interview, the videographer may be asked to film the materials while the narrator describes each of them.

Remember to ask for specifics of place names, names of people, and dates or context. Sometimes the narrator's story is so interesting, you can forget to ask for these details.

Try to establish where the narrator was and what his or her connection to the story was at each major point. This will help differentiate firsthand information from reports given by others.

Avoid asking questions beyond the narrator's expertise or about things he or she will not know firsthand.

When a narrator uses acronyms or jargon that the general public is unfamiliar with, ask for explanations, descriptions, spellings, or translations, as appropriate. Your research or specific knowledge may mean you understand what the narrator is saying, but others listening to the interview or reading the transcript probably will not share this knowledge. This can be especially important with military or other government jargon and acronyms that fall into disuse and whose translations can be difficult to recover.

Use body language and eye contact to encourage the narrator's responses. Smiles and nods are often effective. Silence—even uncomfortable silence—is also an effective tool to elicit information. When the narrator finishes responding to a question, resist the temptation to jump right in with a follow-up or a new topic. Some narrators simply need a few moments to continue gathering their thoughts. Additionally, a natural tendency to want to fill silences in conversation may induce the narrator to add something more without verbal prompting. Repeated verbal encouragement by the interviewer, such as "uh-huh," is intrusive and lowers the sound quality of the interview.

Discourage requests to turn off the recorder. Only information given during the recorded interview will become part of the historical record. If a narrator asks

you to stop the recorder, it helps to see if you can determine what concerns the narrator may have that affect his or her willingness to speak on the record. But if the narrator requests repeated breaks in the recording, you might need to reconsider whether he or she is having second thoughts about participating in the project. Halting the interview for further discussions or clarifications with the narrator about options for closing the interview transcript might be useful. You will have to be prepared to make these decisions on the spot.

Take breaks. This can be done when changing recording media. Allow time to stretch, leave the room, get a drink of water, or quickly review the topics to be covered in the next part of the interview coming up. If a narrator becomes too tired to continue effectively, determine whether you can return for another interview session at a different time. Be sensitive to such situations and handle them graciously.

Use a notebook to keep track of follow-up questions, additional points to make, or other interview needs. This will help keep you organized and will allow you to continue to concentrate on the narrator.

Also use your notebook to keep a running list of proper names mentioned in the interview. It is a good idea to ask the narrator to review this list and correct any spelling errors at the end of the interview. This list should be kept in the master file, with a copy given to the processor.

Keep track of the time. Make sure you don't extend the interview past a reasonable limit.

Immediately label all the recording media. Include the oral history project name, the name of the narrator, the name of the interviewer, the date, and, if appropriate, the media number (for example, "1 of 3 generated in the interview").

Take a photograph of the narrator in the interview setting. This should be done for both audio and video interviews.

Sign the donor form with the narrator. This should be done even if you plan more sessions with him or her.

TROUBLESHOOTING THE ORAL HISTORY INTERVIEW

Narrators sometimes will not immediately give long answers to questions. In such cases, it helps to wait before asking the next question, making sure he or she is not considering an additional comment. If nothing is forthcoming, it may be that the narrator is not interested in or comfortable with the question, and you might try switching to a different topic or approach. It also may be that the narrator isn't sure what kind of additional information you might find interesting, in which case a follow-up question might open the floodgates.

As the interview progresses, the narrator, understanding the direction of the questions, may anticipate several points on the interview outline and cover them with one answer. You will want to be prepared with follow-up questions if necessary. Or, if the information is complete, move to another subject.

Some people habitually answer with short sentences or one or two words. Try to ask questions that elicit as much information as possible, but remember that each narrator is unique and treat the situation respectfully. Verbally interpret nonverbal responses, especially in audio interviews. A brief "I see that you nodded *yes* to my question" will help clarify the situation.

On the other hand, some narrators talk a great deal. A good interviewer is prepared to keep the interview focused on the topics at hand in a polite and gentle manner. Although it is generally better to avoid unnecessarily interrupting, interviewers should be prepared to ask a question at an appropriate moment, such as when the narrator changes the subject.

At times, an interviewer may arrive as scheduled only to discover that the narrator has changed his or her mind about participating for any of a variety of reasons—the narrator's health is not good, the time scheduled for the interview is not good, the narrator is unexpectedly busy, the health of family members is not good, and the like. Interviewers should remain flexible, review the situation, and come up with a solution, which may be as easy as rescheduling.

Narrators also might be unwilling to be interviewed for a variety of other reasons. The topics to be covered, while important to the project, may be irritating or difficult for the narrator to discuss. In some cases, talking about past events or people to whom the narrator was close can bring about emotional reactions. Be prepared for these eventualities. Oral history interviews, while sometimes difficult, offer the narrator a chance to tell fully his or her story and to contribute information about people important to him or her. Often, allowing the narrator a moment of silence or sadness before moving on to happier memories allows you to complete the interview successfully.

ENDING THE INTERVIEW

Ending an interview is an art in itself. Oral history interviews are intense and can involve revelation of extremely personal information. To help the narrator wind down, the interviewer might ask a few introspective questions while giving the narrator an opportunity to add any thoughts or information that might not have been covered elsewhere. Be sure to thank the narrator before the recorder is turned off.

After signing the donor form, which should be done after every interview session, the interviewer may want to sit and talk for a little while to help the narrator unwind. This often depends on how tired the narrator is and the interviewer's schedule. This is the time to ask the narrator exactly how to record his or her name on project files. Sometimes, this is the time for the coffee or tea you couldn't accept during the interview. A measured packing up of interview equipment also allows for after-interview comments and discussion. Another good end-of-interview activity is to review the spelling of proper names jotted down during the interview. While a good exercise for interviewer and narrator, it also provides helpful information for people processing the interview. If this isn't done at the end of the interview, you will want to call the narrator as soon as possible to review and check this information.

Narrators often have photos, other archival material, or artifacts related to the information discussed. If so, they may want either to give the items to the repository holding the oral history project or to loan them for copying (especially in the case of photographs). If project planning calls for taking this information at the time of the interview, carefully inventory all materials, signing and giving one copy of the inventory to the narrator while keeping the other with interview records. If the materials are to be identified for future consideration, the interviewer will still want to look them over and write a description for project coordinators. See Appendix A for sample inventory forms.

Sometimes, during discussions after the interview, a narrator remembers something pertinent to the interview. If possible, you should try to record this information, even if it means unpacking the recorder and setting it up again. As an alternative to this, you can take thorough notes and ask the narrator to schedule another interview session.

Finally, be prepared to answer any questions the narrator might have about the project repository, accessibility, and future use of the interview. If full transcription is to be done, let the narrator know he or she will receive a copy to review and correct before it is put into final form. It is also a good idea to offer the narrator a personal copy of the interview media, explaining when they will be sent.

SPECIAL INTERVIEWING CONSIDERATIONS

Video Interviews

The techniques and guidelines listed above apply to all oral history interviews, whether they are audio or video recorded. But video interviewers should keep in mind the special points related to the physical set-up, as outlined in Chapter Six, as well as these additional considerations.

Remember that a video recorded oral history interview is not a polished documentary program ready for use on television. It is a video version of an audio interview. As such, its focus is on collecting the information as the narrator tells it. Although the video adds a more formal touch to the process, narrator and interviewer should not feel constrained by the presence of the camera. The narrator should be free to start and stop talking in a relaxed manner, including false starts. Do not abandon the use of silences or pauses, though they are more noticeable because of the camera.

More time constraints can affect the use of video compared to audio if recording is done in a studio or on location. It can be easier for the audio interviewer to go a little beyond the allotted one or one and a half hours if the situation calls for it, while camera and studio time are usually rented by the hour and may be tightly scheduled. Because of this, the interviewer should keep an even closer eye on the time during a video interview, making sure to cover the most important or critical information first. Video interviews conducted outside a studio may allow the same flexibility as an audio-only interview.

Telephone Interviews

You may find you need to conduct an interview by telephone. This should be done with care and planning and only if necessary. Time restrictions in a telephone interview can result in forcing it to move at too fast a pace, and it is much more difficult for most people to develop personal rapport over the telephone than face-to-face. Telephone interviews may suffer from the interviewer's inability to read body language and verbal cues, like sarcasm or facetiousness, all of which may affect understanding of the narrator's meaning.

Sometimes, however, a telephone interview may be better than no interview at all, if limited funds prevent traveling to a narrator's location or if the narrator's infirmity or other considerations make a face-to-face interview impossible to arrange. If that's the case, and you must interview by phone, it's a good idea to practice with your equipment in a trial run to be sure the connections will result in an appropriate-quality voice recording. One positive aspect of a telephone interview may be that the interviewer will feel less constrained about taking notes to keep track of follow-up questions and the like, for the note-taking is unlikely to be a distraction the way it might be in person.

E-mail Interviews

We have just one recommendation about the advisability of conducting e-mail interviews: Don't. An e-mail exchange is, by definition, not an oral history interview. It is a more formal, written exchange of information, even more impersonal than a telephone interview. Sending written questions and reading written responses incorporates none of the spontaneity of a spoken exchange and involves no opportunity for the interviewer to take nonverbal cues from the narrator. Moreover, the interviewer cannot even be certain who is providing the answers to the questions.

Having said that, however, one striking exception to this advice is worth noting. Interviewer Esther Ehrlich and playwright and performance artist Neil Marcus created a remarkable interview for the Artists with Disabilities Oral History Project at the University of California, Berkeley Regional Oral History Office, communicating by voice, computer instant messaging, and gestures. Marcus was a child when he was diagnosed with dystonia, a severe neurological disorder that makes it difficult for him to speak and to control his body. To conduct the interview, two computers were set up side by side so Marcus could type responses to Ehrlich's questions, in addition to offering verbal responses from time to time. The interview sessions, six in all totaling sixteen hours, also were videotaped.[4] The critical point here is that Ehrlich and Marcus were engaged in a face-to-face exchange, a defining element of oral history. Use of the computer, as well as their voices, was simply the medium that made the process work, just as sign language may be the appropriate medium in an oral history interview with a deaf or hearing-impaired narrator.

In the absence of such unique circumstances, don't entertain the fiction that an e-mail exchange is an oral history interview. It may be an exchange of information, even historical information, but it is not oral history. If for any reason information gathered from someone in this way is included in an oral history collection, its origins should be clearly defined and explained.

Interviews with Multiple Narrators

It is usually best to interview one person at a time and to have as few people in the room as possible during the process. An interview is an intense situation because of the degree of concentration required by both the interviewer and the narrator, and narrators tend to be more comfortable with fewer people around, although some cultures may require or encourage witnesses or observers.

If you are interested in interviewing several people together, you will want to consider using video. Think carefully, however, about what this interview will produce. Despite the ideal give-and-take that having several people in a group seems to offer, what generally happens is that one person dominates or the narrators contradict one another enough to bog down the interview. Sometimes, even if people disagree with one another they won't say so for fear of offending or being ridiculed by the more outspoken members of the group. It takes an experienced interviewer to keep an interview with multiple narrators moving along effectively.

If interviewing several people together is necessary because of time or other constraints, it is critically important for the interviewer to establish some method of carefully tracking who is speaking if the interview is not video recorded. Many voices sound similar when recorded, and without a running list of the order in which people spoke, or a rule that everyone introduces himself or herself when beginning to talk, a person trying to transcribe such a multi-voice interview session will become hopelessly lost.

Getting groups together and recording their conversations, prompted by an interviewer or group leader, has enjoyed certain popularity at gatherings like college reunions and other similar events. But these might more accurately be called recorded group discussions, not oral history interviews, unless the session has some pre-planned, research-based structure, the participants all sign deeds of gift, and the recording is processed and archived in such a way that the information is available to others.

Traumatic Event Interviewing

Natural disasters like Hurricane Katrina and flooding in the Upper Midwest as well as man-made tragedies like the September 11, 2001, attacks on the Pentagon and World Trade Center, the internment of Japanese Americans during World War II, and the Holocaust have focused attention on the unique needs of those interested in conducting oral history interviews related to traumatic events. Such oral history projects should be approached carefully, with sufficient training for interviewers who may be dealing with emotionally fragile people. A narrator grieving over the loss of a family pet in a natural disaster would not, for example, want to hear an interviewer say she can always get a new parakeet. Nor would it likely be comforting for a narrator to hear an interviewer say, "I know just how you feel."

People who agree to be interviewed in the wake of a personal or public tragedy may instinctively perceive there is a therapeutic value for them in talking about their experiences, and many consider it constructive rather than distressing to do so.[5] But oral historians generally are not trained as grief counselors or therapists, nor are they social workers who can offer to help people put their lives back together. So appropriate backgrounding is a must, as well as appropriate support for interviewers who themselves may experience grief from interviewing the grief-stricken.

Projects that emerge in the immediate aftermath of a tragedy often bear a closer resemblance to journalism than oral history. But unlike journalistic interviews, which are often ephemeral and conducted for immediate publication, oral history interviews of trauma survivors, like the hundreds of interviews conducted by oral historians from Columbia University after the September 11 terrorist attacks, can become a treasure trove of information that scholars will continue to find invaluable.

While some oral history projects intentionally set out to document the experiences of people affected by a disaster, it is important to note that not all narrators may consider themselves victims, regardless of how outsiders may wish to portray them. Moreover, oral history interviewers in projects unrelated to public disasters can unexpectedly encounter narrators who are suffering from private traumas, sometimes decades old, like people who over-mortgaged the family farm and then lost it in the economic turmoil of the 1980s. The emotions of such narrators, while related to personal or family tragedies, are no less real than those of survivors of high-profile public tragedies. Oral history interviewers sometimes encounter such situations and need to be prepared to respond appropriately.

Cross-cultural Interviewing

The 1970 U.S. Census found that a record low 4.7 percent of the nation's population were foreign born. By

2006, the most recent year for which figures are available, that proportion had mushroomed to 12.5 percent foreign born. Moreover, nearly 20 percent of the nation's population over the age of five spoke a language other than English at home.[6] It is no wonder, then, that scholars and community historians have increasingly begun to examine the growing multicultural population and to document the experiences of diverse communities. In fact, James E. Fogerty of the Minnesota Historical Society has noted that if future scholars want reliable information beyond census data on the Hispanic, Asian Indian, Hmong, Cambodian, Somali, or Bosnian communities that are growing segments of that state's population, they "must employ oral history as a documentary tool of major importance."[7]

For oral historians, multicultural projects raise important issues at all stages, from project planning and development through processing of oral history materials.[8]

Language barriers, for example, may pose the first challenge. If the project is initiated by a predominantly English-speaking group, how will representatives most effectively obtain the cooperation and participation of non-English-speaking members of the community? Ethnographer Michael H. Agar talks about connecting with official or unofficial "stranger-handlers" who can introduce outsiders to a group and serve as an informal intermediary to build relationships between the stranger and the group members, a concept oral history project planners might find useful.[9] Beyond the planning process, language issues also need to be considered in writing donor forms, assuring complete explanation of the project to potential narrators, conducting the interviews, and processing all the interview materials. Will the project hire translators? Work with volunteers? Family members? Is it appropriate to use family members? If the translators are not professional translators, what kind of training is necessary to assure they understand that the interviewer wants to know exactly what the narrator said, unedited by the translator? Is it even appropriate for outsiders—the people Agar calls "professional strangers"—to be involved?[10]

Possible language barriers are just one element of the large array of cultural differences that a multicultural oral history project may encounter. Making sure project participants are aware of such differences is an important part of the training process. How—or whether—people shake hands, how close they stand to another person, whether or how they make eye con-

tact, how they use gestures, whether they touch other people, how they treat silences in conversation, whether an exchange of token gifts is expected, even how they smile or laugh are all aspects of nonverbal communication that can vary from culture to culture and within a culture. And if the meaning of such behaviors is not understood—or is incorrectly assumed to be universal—oral history interviews could turn disastrous.

One possible solution is to find people in the communities in which you wish to conduct oral history work who are willing to teach you what you need to know to work effectively toward a common goal. Cultural differences aside, sincere interest and mutual respect go a long way toward overcoming barriers to interpersonal communications.

The challenges associated with planning and carrying out a cross-cultural oral history project are not new. The Depression-era Federal Writers Project, while not a true oral history project by contemporary standards, generated some 2,300 interviews with former slaves that mainly focused on black folklore and songs, but that also included historical questions largely dealing with the narrators' day-to-day lives. Some of the interviewers were black, but many were not, and because whites in the 1930s South widely considered African Americans inferior, the race of the interviewer was part of the unspoken communication underlying all of the interviews.[11]

Some studies of the interviews, the accounts of which are largely based on interviewer notes, not recordings, offer revealing insights into the effect of the unequal power relationships between interviewer and narrator. Some former slaves were quite open about the fact that they weren't being candid in their remarks, as in this excerpt: "Oh, I know your father en your grandfather en all of dem. Bless Mercy, child, I don't want to tell you nothin' but what to please you."[12] Some of the former slaves assumed their white interviewers were connected with the local welfare office, which suggests they were likely to try to ingratiate themselves with the interviewers in hope of receiving assistance. Scholars who have studied the former-slave interviews have been able to identify at least one elderly woman who was interviewed by two different people—one a white woman and the other a black man. The interviewers' versions offer strikingly different accounts of family relationships, white paternalism, and treatment by white slave owners.[13] The differences in the two interviews, in fact, provide as much information about the nature of the relationship between the interviewers and narrator as they do about the details of the former slave's life.

The United States has a centuries-old history of black people and white people being unable to interact with each other with openness and candor, which is clear in the Depression-era interviews.[14] That history can pose a challenge for contemporary oral historians, too, as they embark on multicultural projects.

Here's how one such situation unfolded. A young white woman in a small Midwestern city eagerly sought to interview an elderly black woman, the granddaughter of slaves, as part of a fledgling community African American history project. The interviewer and narrator were acquainted with one another, but the first time they recorded a formal oral history interview, it became clear that topics having to do with racial issues were difficult for them to discuss. When telling a story about her grandmother's childhood, for example, the elderly woman said: "Well, I'll skip that." Likewise, the interviewer passed up opportunities to ask follow-up questions about the elderly woman's schooling, jobs, relationships with young people of other races, episodes in the community involving the Ku Klux Klan, and so forth.

After critiquing the first interview, the young interviewer came to terms with her own discomfort in talking about race with an elderly woman whom she deeply respected. She wrote an introduction to the next interview, and recorded it at the beginning of their next session, in which she stressed the unique contribution the elderly woman could make by being willing and able to tell about what it was like to be a young African American girl growing up in this small Midwestern city in the early 1900s. The community and the state, the interviewer said, were "extremely lucky to be able to listen to you and have a record of this part of the state's history, which was entrenched with institutional racism. You can teach us what it was like, and we can put together a document for others to learn from and gain a better understanding of what it was like for you to grow up here."

Then she described frankly, on the record, the differences between them and the impact that might have on their interview:

It is hard to talk about racial issues sometimes. It may be difficult for me to ask you certain questions, and difficult for you to answer, but I hope we can try. It may be easier for you to talk about the racism you encountered or observed with another African American woman. I can try to set that up . . . but right now I am available and would like to see what you and I can accomplish. A few positive things you and I have together is that we know each other, trust each other, and respect each other. We are both women that like to talk about our lives, and we are friends.

The result? Greater candor by the elderly narrator about subtle and overt forms of racism in the community and more willingness by the interviewer to ask questions about a concealed past.

This episode also serves to illustrate that oral history is not a natural science. It is an intense interaction between two specific people. And those people can never stop being who they are—men or women, black or white, young or old. At one level, every interview is a cross-cultural interview because racial, nationality, or ethnic differences are not the only forms of cultural identity, in its broadest sense. People also make distinctions among one another based on age, socioeconomic level, job status, education level, religion, political affiliations, family connections, and other such characteristics. Thus each combination of narrator and interviewer results in a unique oral history interview. And that's why it's important to document fully all the variables that might affect future users' interpretations of the interview.

Project coordinators should try to pair narrators with interviewers to whom they will respond best. Is a twenty-something with body piercings and tattoos likely to be the most effective interviewer for a demure octogenarian narrator? Will an interviewer who happens to be an employee of the narrator's business be able to ask probing questions? Will a high school dropout be too intimidated to interview a college professor? Will a college professor be too arrogant to interview a high school dropout? Will a priest be able to interview a rabbi? How about the other way around? Sometimes people's differences can spark lively, informative interviews, while an oral history interview between two old friends often results in an exchange of insider information that others may not understand.[15] Are there any absolutes in this process? No. Interviewers need to be able to approach their narrators with good preparation and a sense of respect for the gift narrators are giving to an oral history project.

WRAPPING IT UP

Narrator and interviewer must sign the donor form after all interviews, regardless of whether they are in audio (including telephone) or video format. As stated in Chapter Four, federal copyright law specifies that the words on the recording are protected by copyright and may not be used without the person's permission.

Send a thank-you letter to the narrator as soon as possible after the interview. It should thank the person for his or her time and reinforce the importance of the information given. See the sample in Appendix A.

Although there is no substitute for thorough research and careful preparation before conducting oral history interviews, we offer this caveat: Be prepared to be flexible.

Retired Arlington County, Virginia, librarian Sara Collins recalled an occasion where an elderly woman came to Arlington on a "last" trip to her hometown and wanted to visit the school she had attended from 1913 to 1915. Collins opened the building, which had since become the Arlington Historical Museum, and an interviewer from the library's oral history program rushed over, recorder in hand. The result was a priceless account of the woman's school days, in which she recalled the arrangement of classrooms, described the daily routine of fetching coal and water, and talked about teachers and classmates she remembered. Flexibility and an experienced interviewer combined with a willing, articulate narrator to capture an unplanned firsthand account of a long-ago era.

Oral history interviews are as unique as the people who give them. Each will represent the narrator and his or her characteristics. As such, interviewing techniques will vary with each interview. A well-prepared interviewer, however, can elicit much information important to the overall project. It is not always easy. The interview can be an intense experience for both interviewer and narrator, but the results are well worth the effort.

NOTES

1. The above description of a model interview format is based on the teaching of Martha Ross, retired from the University of Maryland and a past president of the Oral History Association.

2. Donald A. Ritchie, *Doing Oral History: A Practical Guide,* 2nd ed. (New York, NY: Oxford University Press, 2003):92–93.

3. Alice Hoffman, retired labor historian and past president of the Oral History Association, made this point in response to a panel discussion at the 2006 OHA conference in Little Rock, Arkansas, noting that "within every specific question is hidden its answer."

4. "Lives of Artists with Disabilities Documented in Oral Histories," *Oral History Association Newsletter,* Spring 2007:3. For detailed information about this and other interviews in the Artists with Disabilities Oral History Project, go to http://bancroft.berkeley.edu/ROHO/.

5. Zachary M. Schrag, "Trauma-Based Research Is Less Risky Than Imagined," *Institutional Review Blog,* http://www.institutionalreviewblog.com, posted March 23, 2008, accessed June 5, 2008.

6. For exhaustive information about racial, ethnic, and other populations in the United States and by state and locality, begin at http://www.census.gov/.

7. James E. Fogerty, "Oral History As a Tool in Archival Development, "CITRA (International Conference of the Round Table on Archives)-Reykjavík, 2001, Abstracts, at: http://old.ica.org/citra/reykjavik_eng/abstracts/fogerty.rtf., accessed September 25, 2008. Fogerty also notes that in addition to its value in documenting immigrant populations, oral history is increasingly important as a documentation tool in general because of "the decreasing percentage of substantive information contained in records—both paper and electronic."

8. Scholarly literature abounds in fields such as cross-cultural communication, conflict resolution, and ethnography, among others, which oral history project planners may find useful if they embark on a multicultural project.

9. Michael H. Agar, *The Professional Stranger: An Informal Introduction to Ethnography* (New York, NY: Academic Press, 1980):85.

10. For a complete discussion of cultural considerations for oral historians working in American Indian communities, see Charles E. Trimble, Barbara W. Sommer, and Mary Kay Quinlan, *The American Indian Oral History Manual: Making Many Voices Heard* (Walnut Creek, CA: Left Coast Press, 2008.)

11. James West Davidson and Mark Hamilton Lytle, *After the Fact: The Art of Historical Detection,* 2nd ed. (New York, NY: Alfred A. Knopf, 1986):190.

12. Davidson and Lytle, *After the Fact: The Art of Historical Detection,* 2nd ed.:191.

13. Davidson and Lytle, *After the Fact: The Art of Historical Detection,* 2nd ed.:191–199.

14. Davidson and Lytle, *After the Fact: The Art of Historical Detection,* 2nd ed.:185.

15. Retired oral historian Martha Ross was fond of advising students that one would usually get a more informative interview if a grandchild interviewed a grandparent rather than having the son or daughter—the middle generation—conduct the interview, because a grandchild and grandparent "share a common adversary."

CHAPTER 8

Processing and Care

What do you do when the interview is over? Interviews are an exciting part of the oral history process. What are the recommended ways to preserve them and help keep them accessible? Processing helps ensure the information they contain will be available for a long time. Working with a repository to provide ongoing curatorial care also can help assure this outcome.[1] This chapter covers processing techniques and provides guidelines for working with a repository.

The first processing step is to use acid-free markers to clearly label the interview media with the name of narrator, interviewer, project, the date, and the media number if more than one is used in an interview. Next, regardless of the type of recording media you are using, a cardinal rule of oral history comes into play. Make backup copies of your interviews to protect them from inadvertent loss. If no other audio exists, make a copy of the audio portion of video footage. Follow the guidelines for storing and backing up data files given in Chapter Five. Immediate preservation can include making copies of the same interviews on several external hard drives and keeping the hard drives in separate rooms or locations until turning them over to the repository—which you will want to do as quickly as possible.

This is the time to check for the possibility, however remote, of potentially defamatory statements in the interview. These sometimes can slip past the most astute interviewer. If found, refer to the information in Chapter Four and check immediately with your contact person at the repository about how to handle the situation.

PROJECT FORMS AND OTHER POST-INTERVIEW TASKS

The period shortly after the interview can be a busy one for the interviewer. This is the time to finish housekeeping tasks:

- Make sure all signatures are on the donor form and it is filed with interview materials.
- Make sure the biography information form is complete. It often is filled out as part of the in-

terview process; now is the time to check it over and fill in any missing information.

- Fill out the interview information form (a sample is included in Appendix A). This is an initial interview processing step. It includes a short outline of the interview along with basic inventory information.
- Check the photo, artifact, and manuscript forms. They contain information about memorabilia such as photographs, scrapbooks, and other materials pertaining to the project. If a narrator has agreed to allow use of materials for the project, the interviewer should develop an itemized list of these materials before leaving the interview, following the instructions on the forms (see Appendix A). This is the time to make sure you have completed the forms and that the lists are accurate. This also is the time to send the narrator a copy of the lists if that has not already been done.
- Review all other interview materials including the question outline used during the interview, correspondence, and materials documenting telephone and personal contacts with the narrator. All paperwork should be ready to turn over to the repository when work on the recording is finished.

This is the time to write up notes about the interview. The interviewer's information and insights help future users of the oral history information understand details about interview context and content. Notes can include comments about the setting, the narrator's reactions to the interview, the narrator's health or other issues that could affect the interview, and speech patterns such as regular use of filled pauses (ums and ahs) or of phrases in more than one language. They need not cover pages; often bullet points are sufficient, but make them as thorough and detailed as possible to provide appropriate context.

This also is the time to check the spelling of proper names on the list made during the interview and to

INTERVIEW INFORMATION FORM

Vietnam Veterans Oral History
(project name)

Narrator Name (as the name appears on the Biographical Information Form)

John Doe

Address *429 1st Street, Laurel, Nebraska*

Interviewer Name *Mary Smith*
Address *549 Oak Street, Barneston, Nebraska*

Date and Place of Interview *October 16, 2008, Lincoln, Nebraska*

Recording Format (check all that apply):
Video: VHS___ DVD _✓_ Other (specify)_____
Audio: Cassette___ Digital (specify) *sound card*
Length of Interview *1.5* (hrs) Master file location *State University archives*
Transferred to Electronic Storage (Master Server/Transfer Date) *State U / 2/28/09*
_✓_External Hard Drive ___DVD _✓_CD _____Other (specify)

Oral History Donor Form Signed *10/16/08* (Date) Unrestricted _✓_ Restricted___
Transcript *12/2/08* (date)   Reviewed by Narrator *1/21/09* (date)

Interview Abstract

- Doe started by describing his decision to enlist in Marines fairly late in Vietnam War
- Discusses training, selection for embassy guard duty
- Discusses conditions upon arrival in Saigon
- Describes relationships with South Vietnamese civilians, especially those working at embassy
- Describes chaos of final days of war
- Among last people to leave embassy
- Reflects on reactions to homecoming; family welcomed him, publicly got cold shoulder

Master recording on State U's master server. One additional copy on external hard drive in State U archives. Two CDs for researchers @ State U archives.

Form Filled Out By *Mary Smith*
Date *2/28/09*

Figure 8.1.   An example of a filled-out Interview Information Form.

make a copy of this list for the transcriber to use when transcribing the interview. And, of course, this is the time to write a thank-you letter to the narrator.

RECORDING ABSTRACT

A recording abstract is an annotated list of the topics covered in the interview. Although not as time-consuming to develop as a transcript, it still takes time. The result is a summary of the interview information rather than a verbatim transcript of the full interview.

Some projects expect their interviewers to perform this task. If that is the plan, make sure interviewers understand it at the outset. Providing a model to work from is helpful. For an example, see figure 8.2.

Developing a recording abstract is a two-step process. The first step is to listen carefully to the full interview and write a concise, detailed one- or two-page summary of the interview information, paying careful attention to correct spelling of all proper names. The second step is to listen to the interview again and, using a watch with a second hand, develop a log in real time—the time elapsed as each new subject is brought up. With each new subject, write a short synopsis of the discussion. Do not include questions, just the narrator's information. Bullet points or phrases rather than complete sentences work well. Attach a complete and correctly spelled list of all proper names mentioned in the interview.

TRANSCRIBING

Transcribing interviews is an often-discussed part of the oral history process. Questions about transcripts generally cover access to and use of interview information. What is oral history—the recording or the verbatim transcript? Which better represents the interview? Which better serves the user? Donald A. Ritchie commented on this issue in *Doing Oral History: A Practical Guide*: "Tape and transcript are two types of records of the same interview. Archivists generally consider the tape, being the original and verbatim record, the primary document. Looked at another way, the tape records what was said and the transcript represents the intended meaning of what was said."[2]

Ideally, the goal for oral history projects is access to the recordings accompanied by verbatim, subject-indexed transcripts. Digital migration techniques offer the possibility of continuing access to recordings, although the reality may not be cost effective for many repositories. Transcripts are archival and reference tools that provide continuing access to interview information. Developed by transcribers trained to accurately capture the nuances of an interview, when printed on acid-free paper and kept in archival conditions, they are a stable format that can keep interview information accessible beyond the life of the media.[3] Transcripts also can be kept as computer files on a server as a backup to the archival paper copies and can be formatted to include metadata that describes the interview and provides access points for searches of materials posted to a website. A time code indicator in real time (not keyed to a recorder counter) can tie the transcript to the recorded interview. Depending on the transcribing process, a time code can be inserted using the transcribing software or added manually using the minute hand on a watch or clock.

> Not all products labeled "acid-free" will be safe to use when caring for oral history materials. Some commercial products, while technically free of acid when developed, may develop acids later. Acid-free materials have a pH between 7.0 and 10.0 and a lignin content of no more than 1 percent.

Transcripts may be developed as part of the oral history project or by the project repository; this decision is part of the planning process. Regardless, they are time-consuming and expensive to create, requiring as many as eight hours of processing time (including all transcribing steps) for each hour of interview time. This is not said as a deterrent to transcribing, only as a guide to help when planning this step in the oral history process.

When plans include transcribing, try to work with someone skilled at translating the spoken word to the written page. The subtleties of sentence structure, paragraph development, and punctuation can be difficult to determine, and incorrect representations can result in misleading or incorrect interpretation of the interview information. Transcribers are an asset to any project. The characteristics of a good transcriber include:

- accurate typing skills
- ability to operate, or learn to operate, the transcribing equipment
- ability to hear electronic sound clearly
- a broad general background that lends itself to understanding the purpose of the interviews, the voices on the recordings, and the meanings of the spoken sentences

SAMPLE INTERVIEW LOG

Fill out for entire interview at approximately 3–5 minute intervals, indicating what is discussed at each interval. For example:

Minutes	Brief Statement of What Was Discussed
0:29	Introductory Statement
1:45	Name and Background
3:32	Discuss location and general layout of Comfrey, Minnesota, a town destroyed in a 1998 tornado
6:54	Describes downtown, ca.1930
9:22	Lists the names of many downtown stores, ca. 1930 General Store, Pearson Drugstore, Johnson Clothing, Rex Liquor and Pool Hall, Comfrey Theater, First National Bank
13:54	Describes Windschel Implement, another downtown store Sold International Harvester farm equipment, Cushman motors, and DeLaval cream separators Affiliated with Kelly-Howe-Thompson chain
17:52	Hotel Comfrey and the Linde family Run by "Grandma" Alice Linde Old railroad hotel, home to many of the town's public school teachers ca. 1930
20:23	Ed Luksik and Irene Linde Luksik, one of Grandma Linde's daughters, owned and ran a drugstore in Pipestone, Minnesota. Mr. Luksik once beat the television show *I've Got A Secret* with his secret—someone with a name that sounded like "Looksick" ran a pharmacy
24:23	Mrs. Mabel Blackman and the Saturday night band concert on Main Street
27:02	The town doctor and Prohibition

Abstract Developed by_____

Date_____

Figure 8.2. Sample Interview Log

- ability to translate the spoken word to the written page with great attention to detail, including successfully determining paragraph and sentence structure, appropriate application of the rules of punctuation, and accurate spelling
- ability to learn a narrator's speech patterns and where breaks or pauses in sentences or thoughts occur, including understanding when to continue a sentence and when to start a new one
- high ethical standards, including understanding not to discuss interview information until the transcript has been approved and the materials placed in the repository
- sensitivity to cultural differences such as education, background, and social standing that can have an impact on translation from oral to written formats

It is helpful to plan a short workshop to introduce transcribers to the project and to the types of interviews it covers. A workshop agenda can include:

- training on transcribing equipment and software
- introduction to the transcribing guide
- review of the transcribers' responsibilities and ethical standards as outlined on the transcribers' form (see Appendix A)

Transcribing Suggestions

Develop a transcribing guide to maintain consistency in transcribing formats.

Make sure you spell all words accurately. Check the spelling of all proper names.

Add full names and titles in brackets the first time they are mentioned. Example: [Senator John] Doe.

Listen carefully. If you can't understand a word or phrase after checking it three times, indicate this on the transcript. Check with the interviewer about missing words or phrases. Sometimes the interviewer or the narrator can fill in the missing information.

It is helpful to put a time code in the left margin of the transcript. This will help readers find the spoken information.

TRANSCRIBING GUIDE

When planning to transcribe, consider developing a transcribing guide to cover the format and style you want to use. Transcribing guides often include:[4]

- Transcript title page format. This should include the narrator's name, project name, interview date, and copyright information. Many also include the interviewer's name.
- Transcript format. This should include the first-page heading, format for identifying the interviewer and narrator, pagination, line spacing (for draft transcripts and the final document), font (typeface) style including use of bold and italics.
- A stylistic approach regarding use of paragraphs. Some oral historians prefer a narrator's comments be presented in one long paragraph, regardless of change in subjects. Others prefer that an extremely long statement be broken into shorter blocks for ease of reading. Paragraphs in oral history transcripts generally are not indented.
- Guidelines for spelling, abbreviations, numbers, and honorifics. What about spelling of proper names and procedures for ensuring accuracy? (Was it Mr. John Smith or Mr. Jon Smythe who was prominently mentioned?). The need to check for correct spelling holds true for interviews done with family members as well. Was Great-grandma's name spelled Anne, Ann, or Anna? Pronunciation is not always a guide here; a name may be pronounced in one way (Anna or—phonetically—Ahna) while spelled in another (Anne).
- Guidelines for identifying people by full names and places by full location. If a full name is not stated, transcribers should include the full name in brackets the first time a person is mentioned. When a town name is mentioned, transcribers should include the name of the state in brackets when first mentioned.
- Guidelines for standardized punctuation. Where should a transcriber insert commas? What about the use of ellipses, dashes, brackets, parentheses, and quotation marks? Transcribers follow accepted guides and standards; it is helpful to choose a standard style and to have a style manual available as a reference for your project.
- A stylistic approach for use of language. How do you want to handle false starts (which can

indicate thought process), filled pauses (ums, ers, ahs), Freudian slips, abrupt changes in subject, and grammatical errors? The goal in transcribing is a truthful representation of the spoken word that respectfully represents the narrator.

- A stylistic approach for persistent mispronunciations, grammatical errors, vernacular speech, and regional speech patterns. Transcripts reflect the interview as accurately as possible, but carefully think through the implications of attempting to replicate in writing mispronunciations, dialect and the like, which almost always can be seen as pejorative. On the other hand, some narrators may specifically request that an interview be transcribed exactly as spoken for cultural reasons.[5]
- An approach and strategy for transcribing indecipherable words. Even the most carefully recorded interview can yield such words or phrases. What is the process you want your transcribers to follow? How will these be handled in the audit-checking and narrator-review process? Transcribers generally listen to a word or phrase at least three times before indicating it is indecipherable. Indecipherable phrases are identified in transcripts by a bracketed statement; narrator review of the transcript can be a help in deciphering these phrases.
- An approach for inserting descriptive information. This kind of information usually is enclosed in brackets. Examples include [laughs], [pounds table], [phone rings]. This convention also is used for noting a break in the interview and for noting mechanical failings or sound intrusions. Example: [noise from jet landing at nearby airport interrupted interview].
- An approach for handling interviews in another language or for interviews that contain words or phrases from another language. Ideally, transcribers of interviews in another language will be fluent in the language. Standard guidelines call for fully transcribing all languages in an interview as well as providing a translation into the dominant language.
- An approach for handling information that may be culturally sensitive, sacred, confidential, or narrator-restricted. Here the ethical standards described in Chapter Four should be clearly and carefully taught to all project transcribers. Project leaders will want to specify guidelines that conform to these standards.
- The use of footnotes or endnotes, both explanatory and reference, to provide additional information or enhance clarity. The style manual will be helpful here.
- A suggested format for developing transcriber's notes documenting the details of the transcribing process for future users.

AUDIT-CHECKING AND TRANSCRIPT PRODUCTION

After a draft of the transcript has been completed, audit-check it for accuracy. This usually is done by the interviewer or transcriber. It involves carefully listening to the interview while reading along on the transcript, marking all necessary corrections. An audit-check helps catch spelling errors, omitted words, misinterpreted words or phrases, indecipherable words or phrases, obvious misspeaking of dates or names by interviewer or narrator, and errors that can occur when the transcriber misinterprets a pause or break in speaking. Make corrections with red ink or pencil if possible, cleanly printing them above the corrected spot or in the page margin with a marked indicator to the location of the correction.

When the audit-check is completed and marked corrections have been made, oral history project leaders or interviewers often send a clean copy of the updated draft to the narrator for further review. As a co-creator of the interview, the narrator can help in the transcription process. A narrator can catch inaccuracies in translating the spoken to the written word as well as check for correct spelling, especially of proper names. Often narrators can decipher previously indecipherable words or phrases. They also can add explanations or detail that enhance the meaning of the interview information. When narrators are asked to review the interview transcript, however, it helps to remember that a transcript of spoken words will not read like a written document. Narrators should resist the urge to edit it; the goal is to have a clean, accurate document that is faithful to the spoken original.[6]

Do not skip narrator review if narrators have limited eyesight or difficulty reading. In such situations, either the interviewer or the transcriber should take the draft transcript to the narrator and slowly read it through, allowing the narrator to indicate necessary corrections.

When all corrections have been made and you have a clean, corrected copy of the transcript, develop an

Sample Page, Audit-Edited Transcript

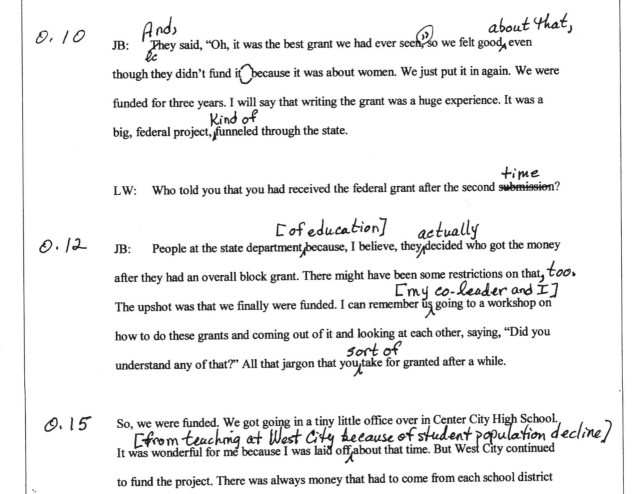

0.10 JB: *And,* They said, "Oh, it was the best grant we had ever seen," so we felt good, *about that,* even

though they didn't fund it because it was about women. We just put it in again. We were

funded for three years. I will say that writing the grant was a huge experience. It was a

big, federal project, *Kind of* funneled through the state.

LW: Who told you that you had received the federal grant after the second ~~submission~~ *time*?

0.12 JB: People at the state department *[of education]*, because, I believe, they *actually* decided who got the money

after they had an overall block grant. There might have been some restrictions on that, *too.*

The upshot was that we finally were funded. I can remember us *[my co-leader and I]* going to a workshop on

how to do these grants and coming out of it and looking at each other, saying, "Did you

understand any of that?" All that jargon that you *sort of* take for granted after a while.

0.15 So, we were funded. We got going in a tiny little office over in Center City High School.

[from teaching at West City because of student population decline]
It was wonderful for me because I was laid off about that time. But West City continued

to fund the project. There was always money that had to come from each school district

as well as federal grant money. They continued to give us support as far as the teachers

and the matching funds. That was a ~~five~~ *three*-year project and was the beginning of our

international women studies project.

Figure 8.3. A page from a transcript showing audit-editing marks.

index. This can be limited to proper names or expanded to include interview topics and concepts. Depending on keyword complexity, the index may be created using word processing programs. Some projects take indexing a step further by compiling individual indexes into a cumulative index covering all project interviews.

Finally, create a title page listing narrator, name of project, date of interview, and copyright information. With the completion of this step, you have created an oral history transcript. See Figures 8.4 and 8.5 for examples.

Make a copy of the subject-indexed transcript and the title page on acid-free paper for deposit with the interview master at the repository. Many projects also send a completed copy to the narrator and make and bind a copy for public use at the repository.

> Consider giving a copy of the recorded interview and a bound copy of the transcript as a gift to the narrator.

GENERAL COMMENTS ABOUT TRANSCRIBING

Transcripts of video interviews may be made from an audio track. Machines or computers with headphone and foot pedal attachments are the most efficient way to transcribe. Playback programs that use computer keys to perform the same functions as foot pedals also are available.

In an attempt to ease initial transcription work, some oral historians have experimented with computer-based voice recognition systems. Questions about the ability of such systems to differentiate among voices in an interview, to understand interviews in multiple languages or dialects, to respond to the subtle nuances of sentence structure, paragraph development, and full punctuation in an oral history interview, and to format a transcript according to the transcription guidelines are among the top factors in determining whether a system will work for an oral history project. Voice recognition systems that may work satisfactorily in business office settings will not necessarily be useful in transcribing oral history interviews. For information about current systems and their applicability for oral history use, contact archivists at your repository, state historical societies, and the Oral History Association.

Transcribing not only can help maintain access to the spoken information, it can also be used as an edu-

cational tool. Interviewers often benefit from transcribing an interview because it focuses concentration on all the parts of the interview from basic structure through follow-up questions. Listening to and analytically observing content and language, especially in one's own interview, can help teach oral history interviewing techniques. It can help interviewers better understand the rhythm of an interview, including what questions sound like, what responses to the narrator sound like, and what common mistakes can sound like.

Transcripts, though not easy to create, help extend the life of the interview information. The bottom line on transcribing always is to do the best you can with the resources you have.

THE REPOSITORY

As discussed in Chapter Three, working with a repository to provide curatorial care from the beginning of the oral history planning process is a critical step. A partnership with a repository helps ensure effective long-term care and accessibility of oral history materials. Project leaders will want to make sure the interviews and all related materials are turned over to the repository as quickly as possible.[7] Related materials may include:

- the original signed donor or legal release form and all other project forms relating to the interview
- the audit-checked transcript with the interviewer's and narrator's comments
- all recorded interview media
- the abstract and interview log
- the transcript printed on acid-free paper, in an acid-free folder and acid-free container, and a computer file copy
- the interviewer's question format and all notes taken in preparation for the interview
- all correspondence between interviewer and narrator, including notes of telephone conversations and copies of e-mail messages
- a photograph of the narrator, often taken in the interview setting, clearly labeled with the narrator's name, the date of the interview, and the project name

Ideally, it is helpful to have a non-circulating master file for each interview. Master files, which usually are not accessible to the public, contain information produced by the interview including the original copy

Interview with John Doe
Interviewed at 123 Ivy Lane,
New City, USA
Interviewed on (date)
New City Oral History Project
Interviewed by Jane Smith

John Doe – JD
Jane Smith – JS

Time Log

0.01   JS: This is Jane Smith with the New City Oral History Project. I am here today to interview John Doe about his experiences in helping develop New City for the project. We are at Mr. Doe's home (address). It is (date). Tell me, Mr. Doe, how did you first become involved with the New City Project?

0.03   JD: I first heard about the project as a student at the State University. I was studying city and urban planning but did not know what I would do with my degree. I didn't want to work for a large city planning firm or for a large city planning department, but those seemed to be the best options at the time. This was during the 1960s and, because of a low number, I was facing the draft. [Note: insert explanatory footnote here explaining the significance of a low number during the Vietnam War draft.] I was talking with one of my professors about my final paper and must have expressed some of my frustration to him. He rummaged around in the papers on his desk and pulled out a flyer about the New City development. It seemed to be just what I was looking for.

           JS: Tell me more about that. Why did it seem to be just what you were looking for?

1.56   JD: It was new and exciting. It seemed to capture the spirit of the times. We all thought, during the 1960s, that we were in a time of new thinking and new ways of looking at things. One of these new ways was how we looked at cities and urban development. The Federal Government had a Model Cities program that was asking many questions as it attempted to develop public policy about urban development. But this program seemed to draw on all the excitement while allowing us to start from scratch in building the perfect city.

Figure 8.4.   Sample Transcript Page with First-Page Heading

**INTERVIEW WITH
JANE DOE**

_____ **ORAL HISTORY PROJECT**

Interviewed by John Smith

Date

© date, ABC Repository

Figure 8.5.   Sample Transcript Cover Page

of the donor form, correspondence, question formats, notes, and the marked copies of the transcript showing narrator's comments. The repository should keep an acid-free original of the subject-indexed transcript or abstract and interview log in an acid-free file folder as part of the narrator's master file. A copy of materials that aid users of the oral history information, such as notes, often is made and kept with a user copy of the transcript.

CARE STANDARDS FOR ORAL HISTORY MATERIALS

As you begin to turn the materials over to the repository, review the storage area if you can and look for details. You will want to reconfirm the care conditions for the oral history materials. Are the storage areas clean? What are the environmental conditions? Recommended standards are:[8]

- Analog tapes available for regular use—65 to 70 degrees Fahrenheit at a relative humidity of 40 to 50 percent with optimum conditions toward the lower end of this range
- Analog tapes in long-term storage—as close to 50 degrees Fahrenheit and 30 percent humidity as possible, but not below this level; allow tapes stored at this level to acclimate to room temperature before use
- CDs—62 to 68 degrees Fahrenheit at about 40 percent relative humidity
- Paper—65 to 70 degrees Fahrenheit at 40 to 50 percent relative humidity

Media should be protected from dust and dirt and stored upright on the narrow edge on archival (not metal) shelving in acid-free containers. Paper materials should be stored in acid-free folders and acid-free containers.[9] See Chapter Five for information about digitizing analog recordings.

What about access policies? What procedures does the repository have in place to prevent loss and damage to oral history materials and to protect them from theft? Generally, access policies include the following:

- a collections access policy identifying the copyright holder, user policies and procedures, permission process for use of materials, and copyright citation guidelines
- a collections access form with a place for name and contact information of user, review of collections access policy information, and place for signature and date

- a master list of all interviews
- a master (non-circulating) file for each interview
- non-circulating, acid-free transcripts with working copies available for users
- separate storage for non-circulating master recordings with working copies available for users
- designated person or position responsible for curatorial care of collection
- supervision of access to collection including designated user areas that are separate from collections storage areas
- use of oral history materials allowed only in designated user areas
- policies for protection of media when handled
- policies for use and control of researcher copies of recordings and transcripts
- standard building surveillance systems including general alarms

For more detailed information on care and maintenance standards, check with your state historical society, your library, or the Society of American Archivists.

Project leaders also will want to be aware of the repository's options for continued access to the media. What are procedures for maintaining media in formats no longer widely available? What about digitizing analog interviews? Does the repository have an ongoing migration plan in place, including digitizing (transferring analog to digital), refreshing (re-creating files on new software-hardware systems), reformatting (moving files to software-hardware systems with different specifications), and migrating (moving data between media)? Technological advances including digitizing analog recordings and recording in "born digital" (interviews that are created and exist only in digital formats) emphasize the importance of a migration plan as a critical factor for ongoing access to the recorded interviews.

The original recording, regardless of type of media, is an archival master; the recommended archival standard is to retain the master in the collections as the original document and to maintain access to it. This includes maintenance of equipment to provide access to the original recordings. It is helpful at this time to confirm that the repository understands and conforms to these guidelines as part of the oral history process.

A word about the Internet. Websites can make oral history information widely available. You will want to decide whether or how to use a website for your project. The discussion of legal and ethical issues related to use of the Internet in Chapter Four provides guidelines for this process. But what about using a website as a repository for your interviews?[10] The proliferation of digital materials makes use of the Internet relatively easy. Do not, however, confuse accessibility with long-term storage. The Internet has expanded access to oral history collections, but it is not a repository.[11] Again, oral history policy guidelines are an important consideration here. Many projects maintain oral history collections in a designated repository and carefully and thoughtfully use websites as optional tools for project information outreach. For more information, see the discussion about Internet use, access, and copyright protection in Chapter Four.

Interview processing and attention to planning for curatorial care of the recordings, while time-consuming and not the most glamorous part of the oral history process, pays years of dividends. It helps ensure ongoing access to the interview information.

NOTES

1. For more information, see the Archivist's Toolkit at http://www.archiveiststoolkit.org, accessed June 26, 2008. Nancy MacKay, *Curating Oral Histories: From Interview to Archive* (Walnut Creek, CA: Left Coast Press, 2007) offers a helpful, step-by-step guide for working with repositories on long-term care for oral history materials.

2. Donald A. Ritchie, *Doing Oral History: A Practical Guide,* 2nd ed. (New York, NY: Oxford University Press, 2003):66.

3. Acid-free materials have a pH between 7.0 and 10.0 and a lignin content of no more than 1 percent. For more information about acid-free standards, see the National Information Standards Organization (NISO), the American National Standards Industry (ANSI), the International Organization of Standardization (ISO), and the Library of Congress. *Archivable Papers: A Report on Acid-Free and Lignin-Free Paper,* http://www.hp.com/sbso/product/supplies/paper/images/acid_lignin.pdf, accessed December 2, 2008.

4. The Minnesota Historical Society Oral History Office "Transcribing, Editing, and Processing Guidelines" has examples of transcript format. http://www.mnhs.org/collections/oralhistory/ohtranscribing.pdf, accessed November 19, 2007. The Institute for Oral History at Baylor University has a "Style Guide for Transcribing Oral History" that provides a comprehensive list of transcript style guidelines from abbreviations to word lists. http://www3.baylor.edu/Oral_History/Styleguiderev.htm, accessed November 19, 2007.

5. Julie Cruikshank wrote of Yukon elders in Alaska who spoke English as a second language and wanted their interviews transcribed exactly as spoken so people in the future could "hear" them. For more information, see Julie Cruikshank, *The Social Life of Stories: Narrative and Knowledge in the Yukon Territory* (Lincoln, NE: University of Nebraska Press, 1998):16.

6. In the context of transcript preparation and review, Linda Shopes commented on the distinction between transcribing (the verbatim record of the interview) and editing (preparing a transcript for further use, such as publication). The oral history process includes transcribing. Linda Shopes, "Transcription Theory, Practice and Politics," H-Oralhist. http://h-net.msu.edu/cgi-bin/logbrowse, July 30, 2002, accessed July 31, 2002.

7. Generally, repositories are libraries and archives in physical locations. Some oral history projects work with digital archives, a "true archive in a digital format." For more information, see Nancy MacKay, *Curating Oral Histories: From Interview to Archive* (Walnut Grove, CA: Left Coast Press, 2007):74.

8. John W. C. Van Bogart, "Magnetic Tape Storage and Handling: A Guide for Libraries and Archives," National Media Library, June 1995. http://www.clir.org/PUBS/reports/pub54, Section 5.2, accessed April 18, 2007. "Technical Glossary of Common Audiovisual Terms: Archival Storage Conditions" http://www.screensound.gov.au/glossary.nsf/Pages/Archival+Storage+Conditions?OpenDocument, accessed April 18, 2007. Michael W. Gilbert, "Digital Media Life Expectancy and Care." http://www.caps-project.org/cache/DigitalMediaLifeExpectancyAndCare.html:6, accessed April 18, 2007. Thomas J. Braun, "Audiotapes and Videotapes," in *Caring for American Indian Objects: A Practical and Cultural Guide,* Sherelyn Ogden, ed. (St. Paul, MN: Minnesota Historical Society, 2004):200.

9. Recordings often require care as they age. For care of analog tapes, see Peter Copeland, *Manual of Analogue Audio Restoration Techniques,* http://www.bl.uk/collections/sound-archive/manual.html, accessed September 16, 2008.

10. A website is an "interface between the information and the user." Nancy MacKay, *Curating Oral Histories: From Interview to Archive* (Walnut Creek, CA: Left Coast Press, 2007):74.

11. For more information, see "Oral History Internet Resources," Columbia University Libraries Oral History Office, http://www.columbia.edu/cu/lweb/indiv/oral/offsite.html, accessed June 27, 2008. Columbia University Oral History Collection, http://library.truman.edu/microforms/columbia_oral_history.htm, accessed June 27, 2008. Regional Oral History Office (ROHO), the Bancroft Library, University of California Berkeley, http://bancroft.berkeley.edu/ROHO/, accessed June 27, 2008. "Oral History Links on the Web," UC Berkeley Library, http://ls.berkeley.edu/dept/ohwg/oh links.html, accessed June 27, 2008.

CHAPTER 9

Making Meanings from Oral History

Are you excited now about the prospect of undertaking an oral history project? Or just overwhelmed? Don't be. Overwhelmed, that is. Creating solid oral history interviews of lasting value is going to require diligent work. But trust us. It will be worth your effort.

The exciting prospects of oral history relate to the first-person information people store in their memories that can supplement, complement, or even challenge information already in the historical record. In some ways, oral histories are much like the Overland Trail diaries of pioneer women that shed light on the daily hardships and wonders of their months on a trail to an unknown land. So also do oral history interviews shed light on soldiers' first hours on Omaha Beach or astronauts' first hours on the moon. Oral histories can be a treasure trove of information about life on a factory floor or in a one-room schoolhouse. Oral histories can explore days gone by in communities large and small and can address the challenge of change, whether man-made or imposed by nature.

Often, in fact, dramatic change sparks an oral history effort. Almost before the rubble settled at the World Trade Center and the fire was extinguished at the Pentagon in the wake of the September 11, 2001, terrorist attacks, oral historians were crafting plans with a journalist's fervor to document the experiences of people affected by the disaster. Sometimes the dramatic change is localized: an organization's benefactor dies; the CEO has a heart attack; the historic district with its run-down but well-loved homes is threatened with demolition for an urban development scheme. And people tied to those organizations or places realize that stories disappeared with the disaster—natural or man-made—and begin planning to capture whatever stories are left. Often there are many. The practical steps described in the previous chapters offer ways to get that process started.

It may not, however, be a disaster that leads to an interest in oral history. Often it's planning for a celebration—the congregation has been here for 150 years, the college is celebrating its centennial, the locally owned business is being passed down to the third generation. Embarking on an oral history project to commemorate such milestones seems a natural thing to do. Again, the information in this manual shows the way.

But in all cases, as oral history has become commonplace in classrooms and community settings of all sorts, it's important to remember that while there may be very real short-term uses for the interviews collected, whether to celebrate an anniversary or fight a zoning proposal or fulfill requirements for a class, an equally important value of the information is simply that it's there for the future, too. When the Cushman Motor Works closed the foundry at its plant in Lincoln, Nebraska, only Charlie Botts could tell us what it was like to be the first black man to move from foundry work—the hardest, hottest place at Cushman—to a job in the tin shop as a welder and sheet-metal finisher.[1] The plant itself is long gone, but an oral history interview with Botts opens a window onto a time and place in the history of race relations in Lincoln as well as work in the factory, which was the initial purpose of the centennial celebration interview. The union-sponsored interviews at Cushman, in fact, resulted in the collection of information that went far beyond what its planners initially intended. They sought to celebrate work by union members on the factory floor. But they also documented stories that contribute to a deeper understanding of race relations, the role of women in the labor force beginning with World War II, changing trends in education, corporate history, workplace health and safety issues, and the globalization of manufacturing, among other themes that emerged from the interviews. In short, it matters that the interviews, created for a specific, short-term purpose, contain information whose value to future generations is unknowable.[2]

Remember the women who laboriously kept diaries on the Overland Trail? Surely they did so for their own unique purposes, probably never imagining the future generations of scholars and history buffs who would collect and publish them and read them for insights into the daily lives of extraordinary but anonymous people who set off to create new lives for themselves and their families. What oral historians can do today as they set off to document something about a time and place they consider important is to consciously document the *context* of their work, a critical element often missing from the written historical record.

While the immediate focus of an oral history project may be a video to show at a centennial celebration or a one-time museum exhibit tied to a civic event, groups and individuals who embark on an oral history project should consider the long-term value of their work to people who aren't even born yet. That's why it's important, if at all possible, to link with a repository that can safeguard oral history materials and keep them accessible for future generations. Moreover, that's why it's important to explain and document in detail the context in which the project was undertaken. What was the frame of reference of those who crafted the mission statement? Who served as advisers? Why were they chosen? What were the circumstances of the interviews? Were some potential areas of inquiry omitted on purpose? If so, why? Oral history project planners need not be defensive about their choices of whom to interview and what topics to cover. But they do need to be open about why they've chosen to proceed as they have. If, for example, community organizing is an overt purpose of a project, planners should say so. That might lead future users of the oral histories to view with skepticism some of the topics or the focus of the work, and it may limit the future usefulness of the oral histories. But as long as everyone associated with the project knows what participants hope to accomplish, in a narrow, immediate sense, the work may still have meaning. The point is to be honest about the purpose of the project and to convey that purpose openly so that future users of the oral histories understand the context in which they were created.

In academic circles, oral history is generally considered a research methodology rather than a discipline, for it does not encompass a specific content area like archaeology or English literature or botany. And as a research methodology, oral history lends itself to use in many settings both within and without the walls of academe.

It is, in fact, the variety of uses to which oral history methods can be applied that make it so exciting—and occasionally frustrating. Oral history materials are frequently used to:

- create museum exhibits,
- narrate neighborhood tours,

- provide raw materials for poetry, songs, dances, and theatrical presentations of all kinds,
- inspire banners, quilts, and other three-dimensional objects,
- document and interpret historic neighborhoods and other historic sites,
- create websites incorporating oral history materials that range from interview summaries and indexes to full-text transcripts and audio or video clips as well as links to related information,
- contribute to natural resources management,
- support genealogy or family research,
- document community history, particularly including the perspectives of historically underrepresented groups,
- serve as a method for gerontologists and others who work with the aged to engage in life review or other therapeutic techniques,
- preserve vanishing languages,
- enliven the study of history in elementary and secondary classrooms,
- contribute primary sources of information for scholarly articles, books, dissertations and the like.

All of these oral history applications, in fact, can occasionally interact in unexpected ways.

An ongoing oral history project at the Suquamish Tribal Cultural Center at the Port Madison (Washington) Indian Reservation, for example, has created an archive of more than 170 oral history interviews that have been used for numerous educational presentations and museum exhibits. They also have been used to identify tribal elders to serve as foster grandparents in the schools and teach children about their native heritage and culture, to provide senior citizen outreach and companionship through home visits, serve as a liaison for social and health services and create jobs for tribal members as researchers, education specialists, museum staff, and work-study staff for tribal college students.[3]

In Minnesota, the Civilian Conservation Corps Documentation Project, which began in 1982, led to a traveling exhibit viewed by more than a million state fair visitors and a book based on the archival interviews. Moreover, an unintended result of the project was creation of a Civilian Conservation Corps museum using excerpts from the oral history interviews as exhibit text.

Archival interviews conducted by the Minnesota Historical Society for an oral history of immigrants from India to Minnesota's Twin Cities have attracted considerable scholarly interest and form the basis of at least one doctoral dissertation by a scholar otherwise unconnected with the work.

In the mid-1980s, the Washington Press Club Foundation created the Women in Journalism Oral History Project, which ultimately completed life interviews with nearly 60 women journalists, ranging from those whose careers began before World War II to those whose careers evolved following passage of the Civil Rights Act of 1964. The archival collection, initially deposited at the National Press Club library in Washington, D.C., Columbia University's Oral History Research Office in New York City, major schools of journalism, and other research libraries, is now available online and has been used extensively by scholars such as journalism historian Maurine H. Beasley. The oral history materials have also been cited in journalism ethics and diversity workshops, and Alexander Street Press, an online publisher of oral history transcripts, among other materials, lists the Women in Journalism collection among the top 100 oral history collections used most frequently.

The Rocky Flats Cold War Museum project in Boulder, Colorado, has completed more than 90 interviews related to the now dismantled nuclear weapons plant and expects to use excerpts from the interviews in museum exhibits. Meanwhile the interviews with former plant workers and people from surrounding communities, including community activists who objected to the nuclear weapons plant's operations, are accessible online to anyone who wants to explore this aspect of Cold War history.

The Immigration History Research Center at the University of Minnesota includes collections of interviews covering 20th-century history of Finnish Americans, Italian Americans, Latvian Americans, and Greek Americans, among others. Most of the interviews are transcribed, and they have been used extensively for master's theses, doctoral dissertations, seminar papers, other scholarly publications, and family histories.

What does this seemingly disparate group of oral history projects have in common? Most of them began many years ago, and some were fashioned *only* as archival projects, that is, no tangible product beyond the archived, transcribed interviews was envisioned at the outset—no website, no stage play, no anniversary celebration. Yet all of them have drawn subsequent generations of scholars, community members, and other interested people who had no hand in creating the interviews, but who have found them valuable primary sources of information that contribute insight to new projects and pursuits.

And that, ultimately, is the magic of creating oral histories. Carefully documented archival oral histories can keep alive the firsthand experiences and knowledge of times and places that otherwise may fade from public memory. When those memories fade, the storehouse of human knowledge is likewise depleted. The steps detailed in the preceding chapters suggest an approach that not only makes it possible to create oral histories that you can use now, for an immediate, short-term purpose, but that also will make it possible for students, scholars, and the just plain curious to open a window onto a time and place outside their realm of experience and come away enriched in ways you may not even be able to imagine. Your oral histories, in other words, are your gift to the future. And the stories you document today will forge a link between a soon-forgotten past and generations yet unborn, enriching the lives of those who tell the stories today as well as those who will hear them, learn from them, and, perhaps, be inspired by them, in years to come.

NOTES

1. Interviews with Charlie Botts and others who worked in the Cushman foundry also illustrate how oral history interviews seldom can stand alone and, indeed, are useful largely in conjunction with background information from other sources. Oddly enough, determining exactly when the foundry closed required sleuthing that involved consulting newspaper archives, corporate archives, and aerial photographs in addition to the recollections of current and retired workers.

2. Laurie Mercier and Madeline Buckendorf, *Using Oral History in Community History Projects* (Carlisle, PA: Oral History Association, 2007).

3. *A Guide for Oral History in the Native American Community*, 3rd ed., developed by the Suquamish Tribal Oral History Project, Suquamish Tribal Cultural Center, Port Madison Indian Reservation, 2000.

Appendix A: Sample Oral History Forms

The following pages provide examples of forms that oral history project coordinators and administrators may find useful.[1]

Sample Narrator Deed of Gift Form with Copyright Language

Sample Interviewer/Recording Operator/Photographer Deed of Gift Form

Sample Letter of Agreement, Volunteer Interviewer

Sample Letter of Agreement, Transcriber

Sample Biographical Information Form

Sample Interview Information Form

Sample Potential Narrator Form

Sample Master Oral History Project Log Form

Sample Photograph Inventory Form

Sample Artifact Inventory Form

Sample Manuscript Inventory Form

Sample Correspondence: Initial Contact Letter

Sample Correspondence: Interview Confirmation Letter

Sample Correspondence: Thank You Letter

[1] A version of these forms also may be found in *The American Indian Oral History Manual: Making Many Voices Heard* by Charles E. Trimble, Barbara W. Sommer and Mary Kay Quinlan (Walnut Creek, CA: Left Coast Press, 2008).

SAMPLE NARRATOR DEED OF GIFT FORM WITH COPYRIGHT LANGUAGE (ALSO CALLED DONOR FORM OR LEGAL RELEASE FORM)

Note: Sign this form at the end of every interview, even if another interview with the narrator is planned.

I, _____ (name of narrator), hereby give to the
_____ (repository) as a donation this interview recorded on
_____ (date). With this gift, I hereby transfer to the
_____ (repository) legal title and all literary rights to the interview, including copyright.

I understand the _____ (repository) may make the interview available for research and use as it may determine, but it may not be broadcast, cablecast, or electronically published for commercial purposes without my written consent. Beyond this, my consent for use has:

_____ no restrictions

_____ restrictions as specified here:

_____

_____

Narrator _____
                                    (signature)

Address _____

City, State, Zip_____

_____

Date _____

Transcript reviewed and accepted by narrator

_____
                (signature)

_____
                  (date)

SAMPLE INTERVIEWER/RECORDING OPERATOR/PHOTOGRAPHER DEED OF GIFT FORM (ALSO CALLED DONOR FORM OR LEGAL RELEASE FORM)

Note: One form must be signed by each individual participating in the recording of the interview. For example, if an interviewer and photographer participate in an interview, each must sign a form. This form must be signed by each individual at the end of every interview, even if another interview with the narrator is planned.

I, _____ (name of interviewer/recording operator/ photographer), hereby give to the _____ (repository) as a donation this interview recorded on _____ (date). With this gift, I hereby transfer to the _____ (repository) legal title and all literary rights to the interview, including copyright.

I understand the _____ (repository) may make the interview available for research and use as it may determine, but it may not be broadcast, cablecast, or electronically published for commercial purposes without my written consent.

Interviewer/Recording Operator/Photographer

_____
                    (one signature per form)
Address _____

City, State, Zip _____

_____

Date _____

SAMPLE LETTER OF AGREEMENT, VOLUNTEER INTERVIEWER

Note: Projects using paid interviewers may want to use a similar form.

I, _____, a volunteer interviewer for the
_____Oral History Project, understand and agree to the following
statements:

- I understand the goals and purposes of this project and understand I am representing the _____
  _____(project sponsor) when I am conducting an interview;

- I have participated in oral history training sessions and am familiar with the recording equipment;

- I understand the legal and ethical considerations regarding the interviews and will communicate them to and
  carry them out with each narrator I interview;

- I am willing to do the necessary preparation, including background research, for each interview I conduct;

- I will treat each narrator with respect and I understand each interview will be conducted in a spirit of openness that
  will allow the narrator to answer all questions as fully and freely as he or she wishes;

- I am aware of the need for confidentiality of interview content until such time as the interviews are released for
  public use per the repository's guidelines and I will not exploit the narrator's story;

- I understand my responsibilities regarding any archival materials or artifacts that the narrator may want to include
  in the interview process; and

- I agree to turn all interview materials over to the repository in a timely manner and to help facilitate all necessary
  processing steps.

_____ Date _____
                     (Interviewer)

_____ Date _____
                (Project Director)

SAMPLE LETTER OF AGREEMENT, TRANSCRIBER

Note: This form may be helpful for use with transcribers, both paid and volunteer.

I,_____, a transcriber for the _____
_____ Oral History Project, understand and agree to the following statements:

- I will provide full, accurate, verbatim transcripts;

- I will follow the specified transcript format, making sure each transcript clearly identifies the narrator, interviewer, and place and date of the interview;

- I will follow the full transcribing process, including:
  - Developing a draft transcript
  - Audit-editing the draft transcript
  - Returning the draft for review
  - Finalizing the draft, correcting any necessary changes, and creating an index
  - Printing the final copy on acid-free paper
  - Providing a copy on disc

- My work will be done in _____ (word processing program) unless otherwise specified;

- I understand the interviewer or project director will provide a list of proper names to facilitate accurate transcribing;

- I understand the interviewer or project director will have 30 days to review draft transcripts and return them for corrections. After that time, they will be considered complete;

- As transcriber, I understand the need for confidentiality of interview content until such time as the interview is released for public use per the repository's guidelines and I will not exploit the narrator's story; and

- I will turn all materials, including copies of the interview recordings and discs containing the transcriptions, over to the repository immediately upon completing the transcribing work.

_____ Date _____
(Transcriber)

_____ Date _____
(Project Director)

SAMPLE BIOGRAPHICAL INFORMATION FORM

Note: A biographical information form keeps track of interviews when they are made and provides narrator background information for future users.

Name _____

Address (home) _____

_____

Address (work) _____

_____

Telephone (home)_____ Telephone (work)_____ E-mail_____

Birth Date and Year_____

Birth Place _____

Occupation _____

Spouse or Closest Living Relative _____

Maiden Name (if applicable) _____

Biographical Information (include information applicable to the interview):

Form filled out by _____

Date _____

SAMPLE INTERVIEW INFORMATION FORM

Note: This form is the first processing step.

_____
(project name)

Narrator Name (as the name appears on the Biographical Information Form)

_____

Address _____

Interviewer Name _____

Address _____

Date and Place of Interview_____

Recording Format (check all that apply):
Video: VHS__ DVD__ Other (specify)_____

Audio: Cassette__ Digital (specify)_____

Length of Interview _____ (hrs) Master file location _____

Transferred to Electronic Storage _____ (Master Server/Transfer Date)

_____ External Hard Drive _____DVD _____CD _____ Other (specify) (check all that apply)

Oral History Donor Form Signed _____(date)
Unrestricted_____
Restricted_____

Transcript _____ (date)   Reviewed by Narrator _____(date)

Interview Abstract

Form filled out by _____

Date _____

SAMPLE POTENTIAL NARRATOR FORM

Note: This form helps keep track of additional potential narrator names as they come up.

_____

(project name)

Name _____

Address _____

_____

Telephone(home)_____ Telephone(work)_____

E-mail_____ Fax_____

Preliminary Narrator Background Information (Describe why this person was suggested as a narrator and what types of information he or she has about the oral history project topics):

Form filled out by _____

Date _____

SAMPLE MASTER ORAL HISTORY PROJECT LOG FORM

Note: This form helps keep track of the oral history project and its interviews.

PROJECT MASTER LOG

Narrator	Interviewer	Interview Date	Release Signed (note type)	Draft Transcript to Narrator	Processing Done (note type and by whom)	Artifacts/ Photos (cross-reference to form)	Put in Repository

SAMPLE PHOTOGRAPH INVENTORY FORM

Note: Narrators sometimes offer photographs for copying or donation as part of the interview process. If that happens, put any photographs you are given for copying or donation in envelopes, *one photograph per envelope,* number the outside of the envelope, and use this form to keep an inventory. Match the numbers on the envelopes to the list below and turn in all photographs in their numbered envelopes, along with this completed form, to the project director immediately after the interview. Give the narrator a completed copy of the photograph inventory form.

Narrator Name (as it appears on the Biographical Information Form)

_____

Address _____

_____

Other Contact Information_____

_____

Photograph #1
Place depicted _____

People in photograph (l to r)_____

_____

Approximate date of photograph _____

Description of photograph _____

_____

_____

_____Loan _____ Donate, date

Photograph #2
Place depicted _____

People in photograph (l to r)_____

_____

Approximate date of photograph _____

Description of photograph _____

_____

_____

_____Loan _____ Donate, date

Photograph #3
Place depicted _____

People in photograph (l to r)_____

_____

Approximate date of photograph _____

Description of photograph _____

_____

_____

_____Loan _____ Donate, date

Continue for each photograph, numbering in order to match the number on the outside of each envelope.

Form filled out by _____

Date _____

SAMPLE ARTIFACT INVENTORY FORM

Note: If the narrator offers artifacts (three-dimensional objects) pertinent to the project, take information about each. Photograph each object and number the photos to match the objects. Turn in all information, along with this completed form, to the project director immediately after the interview. Give the narrator a copy of the completed artifact inventory form.

Narrator Name (as it appears on the Biographical Information Form)
_____

Address _____

_____

Other Contact Information_____

_____

Artifact #1
Approximate date _____

Description (include approximate size, color, composition)
_____

_____

_____

_____Loan _____ Donate, date

Artifact #2
Approximate date _____

Description (include approximate size, color, composition)
_____

_____

_____

_____Loan _____ Donate, date

<u>Artifact #3</u>

Approximate date _____

Description (include approximate size, color, composition)

_____

_____

_____

_____Loan _____ Donate, date

Continue for each object.

Form filled out by _____

Date _____

SAMPLE MANUSCRIPT INVENTORY FORM

Note: Manuscripts and other archival materials, such as letters, diaries, scrapbooks, or other documents, may be offered as part of the interview process. If that happens, put each document you are given for copying or donation in an envelope, *one document per envelope,* and number the outside of the envelope to match the list below. Turn all documents in their numbered envelopes, along with this completed form, in to the project director immediately after the interview. Give the narrator a copy of the completed manuscript inventory form.

Narrator Name (as it appears on the Biographical Information Form)

_____

Address _____

_____

Other Contact Information_____

_____

Manuscript #1
Approximate date _____

Description (include as much information as possible)

_____

_____

_____

_____Loan _____ Donate, date

Manuscript #2
Approximate date _____

Description (include as much information as possible)

_____

_____

_____

_____Loan _____ Donate, date

<u>Manuscript #3</u>
Approximate date _____

Description (include as much information as possible)

_____

_____

_____

_____Loan _____ Donate, date

Continue for each manuscript, numbering in order to match the number on the outside of each envelope.

Form filled out by _____

Date _____

SAMPLE CORRESPONDENCE: INITIAL CONTACT LETTER

Date _____

Dear _____(narrator)

    I am writing to you on behalf of the _____ oral history project. Through this project, we hope to collect information about _____ (project purpose).

    We would like to talk to you about being a part of this project. All interview information will be kept at the _____ (repository).

    One of our project members will call on you soon to talk about this with you and to ask your permission to be interviewed.

    Thank you.

Sincerely yours,

Project Coordinator
_____ Oral History Project

SAMPLE CORRESPONDENCE: INTERVIEW CONFIRMATION LETTER

Date _____

Dear _____ (Narrator)

    Thank you for agreeing to be interviewed for the _____ oral history project. I (we) will come to interview you on _____ (date) at _____ (time and place).

    During the interview, we will talk about:

        List topics to be covered, such as:
- Your background
- Your memories of how you first heard about (topic)
- Your memories of getting started with (topic)
- Your memories of highlights involving (topic)
- Your memories of difficulties involving (topic)
- Your final thoughts and assessment of (topic)

    As part of the interview, I will ask you to give your interview to the _____ _____ (repository). A copy of the interview will be given to you and your family.

    Thank you.

Sincerely yours,

Interviewer

_____ Oral History Project

SAMPLE CORRESPONDENCE: THANK YOU LETTER

Date _____

Dear _____(narrator)

    Thank you for your oral history interview for the _____ oral history project on
_____(date). The information you gave in your interview was very helpful and will be kept at the
_____ (repository).

    A copy of the interview has been made for you and your family. I am delivering it with this letter.

    Thank you again for your time and your information.

Sincerely yours,

Interviewer

_____ Oral History Project

Appendix B: Oral History Association Evaluation Guidelines

Foreword

Since its founding in 1967 the Oral History Association (OHA) has grappled constantly with developing and promoting professional standards for oral historians. This has been no easy task, given the creative, dynamic, and multidisciplinary nature of the field. The OHA has sought to encourage the creation of recorded interviews that are as complete, verifiable, and usable as possible, and to discourage both inadequate interviewing and the misuse of history. Yet it recognizes that oral historians cannot afford to suppress ingenuity and inspiration nor to ignore new developments in scholarship and technology.

The OHA issued its first "goals and guidelines" in 1968, broadly stating the principles, rights, and obligations that all interviewees, interviewers, and sponsoring institutions needed to take into consideration. Then in 1979, at the prompting of various granting agencies, leaders of the OHA met at the Wingspread Conference Center in Racine, Wisconsin, to produce a set of "evaluation guidelines." These guidelines have since provided invaluable assistance to oral history projects of all sizes and purposes. Organized in checklist form, they offered reminders of the myriad of issues involved in conducting, processing, and preserving oral history interviews. Not every guideline applied to every project, but taken together they provided a common ground for dialogue among oral historians.

Over the next decade, new issues arose. When the need for revision of the earlier guidelines became apparent, the OHA decided against convening another special meeting, as done at Wingspread, and instead appointed four committees to examine those sections of the evaluation guidelines that required revision or entirely new material. After a year's work, the committees presented their proposals to the members of the Association at the annual meeting Galveston, Texas, in 1989, where their reports were discussed, amended, and adopted at the general business meeting. During the next year, the chairs of the four evaluation guidelines committees analyzed, revised, and expanded the Goals and Guidelines into a new Statement of Principles and Standards. They offered these standards for amendment and adoption by the membership at the annual meeting in Cambridge, Massachusetts, in November 1990.

If that process sounds convoluted, it was. But its many stages were designed deliberately to foster thoughtful debate among the widest cross-section of oral history practitioners. As a result, the new standards and guidelines more specifically addressed the needs of independent and unaffiliated researchers, as well as those of the larger oral history programs and archives. They dealt with the problems and potentials of videotaped interviews. They raised issues about the use of oral history in the classroom by teachers and students.

The most intense discussions predictably dealt with ethical issues. A greater awareness of the effects of race, class, gender, ethnicity, and culture on interviewing, together with a heightened concern over the impact that the oral history projects might have on the communities in which the interviews were conducted, were woven into both the Evaluation Guidelines and the Statement of Principles and Standards. The new guidelines and standards encouraged oral historians to make their interviews accessible to the community and to consider sharing the rewards and recognition that might result from their projects with their interviewees. They also sanctioned the use of anonymous interviews, although only in "extremely sensitive" circumstances.

During the 1990s, the rapid advances in technology required yet another revision on the new ways of recording, preserving, using and distributing oral history. In 1998 an ad hoc committee presented additional revisions for discussion and adoption by the membership at the annual meeting in Buffalo, New York. These revisions included new sections on recording equipment and tape preservation, and aimed to encourage practitioners to pay more attention to technical standards and to new technology and media, particularly the Internet. At the same time they raised some of the ethical issues that the new technology posed.

All of those who labored in the preparation of the principles and standards and the evaluation guidelines trust that they will offer positive assistance to anyone conducting oral history interviews. While these guidelines and standards provide a basis for peer judgment and review, their success will ultimately depend more on the willingness of the individual oral historians and oral history projects to apply them to their own work.

Donald A. Ritchie

Evaluation Guidelines Committees

1988-1989
Donald A. Ritchie (coordinator), US Senate Historical Office

Committee on Ethical/Legal Guidelines
Sherna B. Gluck (co-chair), California State University Long Beach
Linda Shopes (co-chair), PA Historical & Museum Commission
Albert S. Broussard, Texas A&M University
John A. Neuenschwander, Carthage College

Committee on Independent/Unaffiliated Research
Terry L. Birdwhistell (chair), University of Kentucky
Jo Blatti, Old Independence Regional Museum
Maurice Maryanow
Holly C. Shulman, Washington, DC

Committee on the Use of Videotape
Pamela M. Henson (chair), Smithsonian Institution
David H. Mould, Ohio University
James B. Murray, Shomberg Library
Terri A. Schorzman, Smithsonian Institution
Margaret Robertson, Minnesota Historical Society

Education Committee
George L. Mehaffy (chair)
Patricia Grimmer
Denise Joseph
Rebecca Sharpless, Baylor University
Andor Skotnes, Sage Colleges
Richard Williams, Plum Borough Senior High School

Principles and Standards Committee, 1989-1990
Donald A. Ritchie (chair), US Senate Historical Office
Willa K. Baum, University of California Berkeley
Terry L. Birdwhistell, University of Kentucky
Sherna B. Gluck, California State University Long Beach
Pamela M. Henson, Smithsonian Institution
Linda Shopes, PA Historical & Museum Commission
Ronald E. Marcello (ex officio), University of North Texas
Lila J. Goff (ex officio), Minnesota Historical Society

Technology Update Committee, 1998
Sherna Gluck(chair), California State University Long Beach
Charles Hardy, Westchester University
Marjorie McLellan, Miami University
Roy Rosenzweig, George Mason University

Principles and Standards of
the Oral History Association

The Oral History Association promotes oral history as a method of gathering and preserving historical information through recorded interviews with participants in past events and ways of life. It encourages those who produce and use oral history to recognize certain principles, rights, technical standards, and obligations for the creation and preservation of source material that is authentic, useful, and reliable. These include obligations to the interviewee, to the profession, and to the public, as well as mutual obligations between sponsoring organizations and interviewers.

People with a range of affiliations and sponsors conduct oral history interviews for a variety of purposes: to create archival records, for individual research, for community and institutional projects, and for publications and media productions. While these principles and standards provide a general framework for guiding professional conduct, their application may vary according to the nature of specific oral history projects. Regardless of the purpose of the interviews, oral history should be conducted in the spirit of critical inquiry and social responsibility and with a recognition of the interactive and subjective nature of the enterprise.

Responsibility to Interviewees:

1. Interviewees should be informed of the purposes and procedures of oral history in general and of the aims and anticipated uses of the particular projects to which they are making their contributions.
2. Interviewees should be informed of the mutual rights in the oral history process, such as editing, access restrictions, copyrights, prior use, royalties, and the expected disposition and dissemination of all forms of the record, including the potential for electronic distribution.
3. Interviewees should be informed that they will be asked to sign a legal release. Interviews should remain confidential until interviewees have given permission for their use.
4. Interviewers should guard against making promises to interviewees that the interviewers may not be able to fulfill, such as guarantees of publication and control over the use of interviews after they have been made public. In all future uses, however, good faith efforts should be made to honor the spirit of the interviewee's agreement.
5. Interviews should be conducted in accord with any prior agreements made with the interviewee, and such agreements should be documented for the record.
6. Interviewers should work to achieve a balance between the objectives of the project and the perspectives of the interviewees. They should be sensitive to the diversity of social and cultural experiences and to the implications of race, gender, class, ethnicity, age, religion, and sexual orientation. They should encourage interviewees to respond in their own style and language and to address issues that reflect their concerns. Interviewers should fully explore all appropriate areas of inquiry with the interviewee and not be satisfied with superficial responses.
7. Interviewers should guard against possible exploitation of interviewees and be sensitive to the ways in which their interviews might be used. Interviewers must respect the rights of interviewees to refuse to discuss certain subjects, to restrict access to the interview, or, under Guidelines extreme circumstances, even to choose anonymity. Interviewers should clearly explain these options to all interviewees.
8. Interviewers should use the best recording equipment within their means to accurately reproduce the interviewee's voice and, if appropriate, other sounds as well as visual images.
9. Given the rapid development of new technologies, interviewees should be informed of the wide range of potential uses of their interviews.
10. Good faith efforts should be made to ensure that the uses of recordings and transcripts comply with both the letter and spirit of the interviewee's agreement.

Responsibility to the Public and to the Profession:

1. Oral historians have a responsibility to maintain the highest professional standards in the conduct of their work and to uphold the standards of the various disciplines and professions with which they are affiliated.

2. In recognition of the importance of oral history to an understanding of the past and of the cost and effort involved, interviewers and interviewees should mutually strive to record candid information of lasting value and to make that information accessible.

3. Interviewees should be selected based on the relevance of their experiences to the subject at hand.

4. Interviewers should possess interviewing skills as well as professional competence and knowledge of the subject at hand.

5. Regardless of the specific interests of the project, interviewers should attempt to extend the inquiry beyond the specific focus of the project to create as complete a record as possible for the benefit of others.

6. Interviewers should strive to prompt informative dialogue through challenging and perceptive inquiry. They should be grounded in the background of the persons being interviewed and, when possible, should carefully research appropriate documents and secondary sources related to subjects about which the interviewees can speak.

7. Interviewers should make every effort to record their interviews using the best recording equipment within their means to reproduce accurately the interviewee's voice and, if appropriate, image. They also should collect and record other historical documentation the interviewee may possess, including still photographs, print materials, and other sound and moving image recordings, if appropriate.

8. Interviewers should provide complete documentation of their preparation and methods, including the circumstances of the interviews.

9. Interviewers and, when possible, interviewees should review and evaluate their interviews, including any summaries or transcriptions made from them.

10. With the permission of the interviewees, interviewers should arrange to deposit their interviews in an archival repository that is capable of both preserving the interviews and eventually making them available for general use. Interviewers should provide basic information about the interviews, including project goals, sponsorship, and funding. Preferably, interviewers should work with repositories before conducting the interviews to determine necessary legal Guidelines arrangements. If interviewers arrange to retain first use of the interviews, it should be only for a reasonable time before public use.

11. Interviewers should be sensitive to the communities from which they have collected oral histories, taking care not to reinforce thoughtless stereotypes nor to bring undue notoriety to them. Interviewers should take every effort to make the interviews accessible to the communities.

12. Oral history interviews should be used and cited with the same care and standards applied to other historical sources. Users have a responsibility to retain the integrity of the interviewee's voice, neither misrepresenting the interviewee's words nor taking them out of context.

13. Sources of funding or sponsorship of oral history projects should be made public in all exhibits, media presentations, or publications that result from the projects.

14. Interviewers and oral history programs should conscientiously consider how they might share with interviewees and their communities the rewards and recognition that might result from their work.

<u>Responsibility for Sponsoring and Archival Institutions:</u>
1. Institutions sponsoring and maintaining oral history archives have a responsibility to interviewees, interviewers, the profession, and the public to maintain the highest technical, professional, and ethical standards in the creation and archival preservation of oral history interviews and related materials.

2. Subject to conditions that interviewees set, sponsoring institutions (or individual collectors) have an obligation to: prepare and preserve easily usable records; keep abreast of rapidly developing technologies for preservation and dissemination; keep accurate records of the creation and processing of each interview; and identify, index, and catalog interviews.

3. Sponsoring institutions and archives should make known through a variety of means, including electronic modes of distribution, the existence of interviews open for research.

4. Within the parameters of their missions and resources, archival institutions should collect interviews generated by independent researchers and assist interviewers with the necessary legal agreements.

5. Sponsoring institutions should train interviewers. Such training should: provide them basic instruction in how to record high fidelity interviews and, if appropriate, other sound and moving image recordings; explain

the objectives of the program to them; inform them of all ethical and legal considerations governing an interview; and make clear to interviewers what their obligations are to the program and to the interviewees.

6. Interviewers and interviewees should receive appropriate acknowledgment for their work in all forms of citation or usage.

7. Archives should make good faith efforts to ensure that uses of recordings and transcripts, especially those that employ new technologies, comply with both the letter and spirit of the interviewee's agreement.

Oral History Evaluation Guidelines

Program/Project Guidelines

Purposes and Objectives

    a. Are the purposes clearly set forth? How realistic are they?

    b. What factors demonstrate a significant need for the project?

    c. What is the research design? How clear and realistic is it?

    d. Are the terms, conditions, and objectives of funding clearly made known to judge the potential effect of such funding on the scholarly integrity of the project? Is the allocation of funds adequate to allow the project goals to be accomplished?

    e. How do institutional relationships affect the purposes and objectives?

Selection of Recording Equipment

    a. Should the interview be recorded on sound or visual recording equipment?

    b. Are the best possible recording equipment and media available within one's budget being used?

    c. Are interviews recorded on a medium that meets archival preservation standards?

    d. How well has the interviewer mastered use of the equipment upon which the interview will be recorded?

Selection of Interviewers and Interviewees

    a. In what ways are the interviewers and interviewees appropriate (or inappropriate) to the purposes and objectives?

    b. What are the significant omissions and why were they omitted?

Records and Provenance

    a. What are the policies and provisions for maintaining a record of the provenance of interviews? Are they adequate? What can be done to improve them?

    b. How are records, policies, and procedures made known to interviewers, interviewees, staff, and users?

    c. How does the system of records enhance the usefulness of the interviews and safeguard the rights of those involved?

Availability of Materials

    a. How accurate and specific is the publicizing of the interviews?

    b. How is information about interviews directed to likely users? Have new media and electronic methods of distribution been considered to publicize materials and make them available?

    c. How have the interviews been used?

Finding Aids

    a. What is the overall design for finding aids? Are the finding aids adequate and appropriate?

    b. How available are the finding aids?

    c. Have new technologies been used to develop the most effective finding aids?

Management, Qualifications, and Training

    a. How effective is the management of the program/project?

    b. What are the provisions for supervision and staff review?

    c. What are the qualifications for staff positions?

    d. What are the provisions for systematic and effective training?

    e. What improvements could be made in the management of the program/project?

Ethical/Legal Guidelines

<u>What procedures are followed to assure that interviewers/programs recognize and honor their responsibility to the interviewees? Specifically, what procedures are used to assure that:</u>

    a. The interviewees are made fully aware of the goals and objectives of the oral history program/project?

    b. The interviewees are made fully aware of the various stages of the program/project and the nature of their participation at each stage?

    c. The interviewees are given the opportunity to respond to questions as freely as possible and are not subjected to stereotyped assumptions based on race, ethnicity, gender, class, or any other social/cultural characteristic?

    d. The interviewees understand their rights to refuse to discuss certain subjects, to seal portions of the interviews, or in extremely sensitive circumstances even to chooseto remain anonymous?

    e. The interviewees are fully informed about the potential uses of the material, including deposit of the interviews in a repository, publication in all forms of print or electronic media, including the Internet or other emerging technologies, and all forms of public programming?

    f. The interviewees are provided a full and easily comprehensible explanation of their legal rights before being asked to sign a contract or deed of gift transferring rights, title, and interest in the tape(s) and transcript(s) to an administering authority or individual?

    g. Care is taken so that the distribution and use of the material complies with the letter and spirit of the interviewees' agreements?

    h. All prior agreements made with the interviewees are honored?

    i. The interviewees are fully informed about the potential for and disposition of royalties that might accrue from the use of their interviews, including all forms of public programming?

    j. The interviews and any other related materials will remain confidential until the interviewees have released their contents?

<u>What procedures are followed to assure that interviewers/programs recognize and honor their responsibilities to the profession? Specifically, what procedures assure that:</u>

    a. The interviewer has considered the potential for public programming and research use of the interviews and has endeavored to prevent any exploitation of or harm to interviewees?

    b. The interviewer is well trained to conduct the interview in a professional manner, including the use of appropriate recording equipment and media?

    c. The interviewer is well grounded in the background of the subject(s) to be discussed?

    d. The interview will be conducted in a spirit of critical inquiry and that efforts will be made to provide as complete a historical record as possible?

    e. The interviewees are selected based on the relevance of their experience to the subject at hand and that an appropriatecross-section of interviewees is selected for any particular project?

    f. The interview materials, including recordings, transcripts, relevant photographic, moving image, and sound documents as wellas agreements and documentation of the interview process, will be placed in a repository after a reasonable period of time, subject to the agreements made with the interviewee and that the repository will administer their use in accordance with those agreements?

    g. The methodologies of the program/project, as well as its goals and objectives, are available for the general public to evaluate?

    h. The interview materials have been properly cataloged, including appropriate acknowledgment and credit to the interviewer, and that their availability for research use is made known?

<u>What procedures are followed to assure that interviewers and programs are aware of their mutual responsibilities and obligations? Specifically, what procedures are followed to assure that:</u>

    a. Interviewers are made aware of the program goals and are fully informed of ethical and legal considerations?

    b. Interviewers are fully informed of all the tasks they are expected to complete in an oral history project?

    c. Interviewers are made fully aware of their obligations to the oral history program/sponsoring institution, regardless of their own personal interest in a program/project?

    d. Programs/sponsoring institutions treat their interviewers equitably by providing for appropriate compensation, acknowledging all products resulting from their work, and supporting fieldwork practices consistent with professional standards whenever there is a conflict betweenthe parties to the interview?

e. Interviewers are fully informed of their legal rights and of their responsibilities to both the interviewee and to the sponsoring institution?

<u>What procedures are followed to assure that interviewers and programs recognize and honor their responsibilities to the community/public? Specifically, what procedures assure that:</u>
  a. The oral history materials and all works created from them will be available and accessible to the community that participated in the project?
  b. Sources of extramural funding and sponsorship are clearly noted for each interview of project?
  c. The interviewers and project endeavor not to impose their own values on the community being studied?
  d. The tapes and transcripts will not be used unethically?

Recording Preservation Guidelines
<u>Recognizing the significance of the recording for historical and cultural analysis and the potential uses of oral history interviews in nonprint media, what procedures are followed to assure that:</u>
  a. Appropriate care and storage of the original recordings begins immediately after their creation?
  b. The original recordings are duplicated and stored according to accepted archival standards [i.e. stored in closed boxes in a cool, dry, dust-free environment]?
  c. Original recordings are re-duplicated onto the best preservation media before significant deterioration occurs?
  d. Every effort is made in duplicating tapes to preserve a faithful facsimile of the interviewee's voice?
  e. All transcribing, auditing, and other uses are done from a duplicate, not the original recording?

Tape/Transcript Processing Guidelines
<u>Information about the Participants:</u>
  a. Are the names of both interviewer and interviewee clearly indicated on the tape/abstract/transcript and in catalog materials?
  b. Is there adequate biographical information about both interviewer and interviewee? Where can it be found?

<u>Interview Information</u>
  a. Are the tapes, transcripts, time indices, abstracts, and other materials presented for use identified as to the program/project of which they are a part?
  b. Are the date and place of the interview indicated on the tape, transcript, time index, and abstract and in appropriate catalog material?
  c. Are there interviewers' statements about the preparation for or circumstances of the interviews? Where? Are they generally available to researchers? How are the rights of the interviewees protected against improper use of such commentaries?
  d. Are there records of contracts between the program and the interviewee? How detailed are they? Are they available to researchers? If so, with what safeguards for individual rights and privacy?

<u>Interview Tape Information</u>
  a. Is the complete original tape preserved? Are there one or more duplicate copies?
  b. If the original or any duplicate has been edited, rearranged, cut, or spliced in any way, is there a record of that action, including by whom, when, and for what purposes the action was taken?
  c. Do the tape label and appropriate catalog materials show the recording speed, level, and length of the interview? If videotaped, do the tape label and appropriate catalog information show the format (e.g., U-Matic, VHS, 8mm, etc.) and scanning system and clearly indicate the tracks on which the audio and time code have been recorded?
  d. In the absence of transcripts, are there suitable finding aids to give users access to information on the tapes? What form do they take? Is there a record of who prepared these finding aids?
  e. Are researchers permitted to listen to or view the tapes? Are there any restrictions on the use of the tapes?

<u>Interview Transcript Information</u>
  a. Is the transcript an accurate record of the tape? Is a careful record kept of each step of processing the transcript, including who transcribed, audited, edited, retyped, and proofread the transcripts in final copy?

b. Are the nature and extent of changes in the transcript from the original tape made known to the user?

c. What finding aids have been prepared for the transcript? Are they suitable and adequate? How could they be improved?

d. Are there any restrictions on access to or use of the transcripts? Are they clearly noted?

e. Are there any photo materials or other supporting documents for the interview? Do they enhance and supplement the text?

f. If videotaped, does the transcript contain time references and annotation describing the complementary visuals on the videotape?

Interview Content Guidelines

Does the content of each interview and the cumulative content of the whole collection contribute to accomplishing the objectives of the program/project?

a. In what particulars does each interview or the whole collection succeed or fall short of the objectives of the project or program?

b. Do audio and visual tapes in the collection avoid redundancy and supplement one another in interview content and focus?

In what ways does the program/project contribute to historical understanding?

a. In what particulars does each interview or the whole collection succeed or fall short in making such a contribution?

b. To what extent does the material add fresh information, fill gaps in the existing record, and/or provide fresh insights and perspectives?

c. To what extent is the information reliable and valid? Is it eyewitness or hearsay evidence? How well and in what manner does it meet internal and external tests of corroboration, consistency, and explication of contradictions?

d. What is the relationship of the interview information to existing documentation and historiography?

e. How does the texture of the interview impart detail, richness, and flavor to the historical record?

f. What is the nature of the information contributed? Is it facts, perceptions, interpretations, judgments, or attitudes, and how does each contribute to understanding?

g. Are the scope, volume, and representativeness of the population interviewed appropriate and sufficient to the purpose? Is there enough testimony to validate the evidence without passing the point of diminishing returns? How appropriate is the quantity to the purposes of the study?

h. How do the form and structure of the interviews contribute to making the content understandable?

i. To what extent does the audio and/or video recording capture unique sound and visual information?

j. Do the visual and other sound elements complement and/or supplement the verbal information? Has the interview captured processes, objects, or other individuals in the visual and sound environment?

Interview Conduct Guidelines

Use of Other Sources

a. Is the oral history technique the best way to acquire the information? If not, what other sources exist? Has the interviewer used them and sought to preserve them if necessary?

b. Has the interviewer made an effort to consult other relevant oral histories?

c. Is the interview technique a valuable way to supplement existing sources?

d. Do videotaped interviews complement, not duplicate, existing still or moving visual images?

Interviewer Preparation

a. Is the interviewer well informed about the subjects under discussion?

b. Are the primary and secondary sources used to prepare for the interview adequate?

c. Has the interviewer mastered the use of appropriate recording equipment and the field-recording techniques that insure a high-fidelity recording?

Interviewee Selection and Orientation

    a. Does the interviewee seem appropriate to the subjects discussed?

    b. Does the interviewee understand and respond to the interview purposes?

    c. Has the interviewee prepared for the interview and assisted in the process?

    d. If a group interview, have composition and group dynamics been considered in selecting participants?

Interviewer-Interviewee Relations

    a. Do interviewer and interviewee collaborate with each other toward interview objectives?

    b. Is there a balance between empathy and analytical judgment in the interview?

    c. If videotaped, is the interviewer/interviewee relationship maintained despite the presence of a technical crew? Do the technical personnel understand how a videotaped oral history interview differs from a scripted production?

Technique and Adaptive Skills

    a. In what ways does the interview show that the interviewer has used skills appropriate to the interviewee's condition (health, memory, metal alertness, ability to communicate, time schedule, etc.) and the interview location and conditions (disruptions and interruptions, equipment problems, extraneous participants, background noises, etc.)?

    b. What evidence is there that the interviewer has thoroughly explored pertinent lines of thought? Followed up on significant clues? Made an effort to identify sources of information? Employed critical challenges when needed? Thoroughly explored the potential of the visual environment, if videotaped?

    c. Has the progam/project used recording equipment and media that are appropriate for the purposes of the work and potential nonprint as well as print uses of the material? Are the recordings of the highest appropriate technical quality? How could they be improved?

    d. If videotaped, are lighting, composition, camera work, and sound of the highest appropriate technical quality?

    e. In the balance between content and technical quality, is the technical quality good without subordinating the interview process?

Perspective

    a. Do the biases of the interviewer interfere with or influence the responses of the interviewee?

    b. What information is available that may inform the users of any prior or separate relationship between the interviewer and interviewee?

Historical Contribution

    a. Does the interviewer pursue the inquiry with historical integrity?

    b. Do other purposes being served by the interview enrich or diminish quality?

    c. What does the interview contribute to the larger context of historical knowledge and understanding?

Independent/Unaffiliated Researcher Guidelines

Creation and Use of Interviews

    a. Has the independent/unaffiliated researcher followed the guidelines for obtaining interviews as suggested in the Program/Project Guideline section?

    b. Have proper citation and documentation been provided in works created (books, articles, audio-visual productions, or other public presentations) to inform users of the work about the interviews used and the permanent location of the interviews?

    c. Do works created include an explanation of the interview project, including editorial procedures?

    d. Has the independent/unaffiliated researcher arranged to deposit the works created in an appropriate repository?

Transfer of Interviews to Archival Repository

    a. Has the independent/unaffiliated researcher properly obtained the agreement of the repository before making representations about the disposition of the interviews?

b. Is the transfer consistent with agreements or understandings with interviewees? Were legal agreements obtained from interviewees?

c. Has the researcher provided the repository with adequate descriptions of the creation of the interviews and the project?

d. What is the technical quality of the recorded interviews? Are the interviews transcribed, abstracted, or indexed, and, if so, what is the quality?

Educator and Student Guidelines

Has the educator:

a. Become familiar with the "Oral History Evaluation Guidelines" and conveyed their substance to the student?

b. Ensured that each student is properly prepared before going into the community to conduct oral history interviews, including familiarization with the ethical issues surrounding oral history and the obligation to seek the informed consent of the interviewee?

c. Become familiar with the literature, recording equipment, techniques, and processes of oral history so that the best possible instruction can be presented to the student?

d. Worked with other professionals and organizations to provide the best oral history experience for the student?

e. Considered that the project may merit preservation and worked with other professionals and repositories to preserve and disseminate these collected materials?

f. Shown willingness to share expertise with other educators, associations, and organizations?

Has the student:

a. Become thoroughly familiar with the equipment, techniques, and processes of oral history interviewing and the development of research using oral history interviews?

b. Explained to the interviewee the purpose of the interview and how it will be used and obtained the interviewee's informed consent to participate?

c. Treated the interviewee with respect?

d. Signed a receipt for and returned any materials borrowed from the interviewee?

e. Obtained a signed legal release for the interview?

f. Kept her/his word about oral or written promises made to the interviewee?

g. Given proper credit (oral or written) when using oral testimony and used the material in context?

Bibliography

Allen, Barbara, and William Lynwood Montell. *From Memory to History: Using Oral Sources in Local Historical Research.* Nashville: American Association for State and Local History, 1981.

Baum, Willa K. *Oral History for the Local Historical Society* Revised edition. Nashville: American Association for State and Local History, 1987.

————. *Transcribing and Editing Oral History.* Nashville: American Association for State and Local History, 1977.

Brecher, Jeremy. *History from Below: How to Uncover and Tell the Story of Your Community, Association, or Union.* New Haven, Conn.: Commonwork Pamphlets/Advocate Press, 1986.

Charlton, Thomas L. *Oral History for Texans* 2d ed. Austin: Texas Historical Commission, 1985.

Davis, Cullom, et al. . Chicago: American Library Association, 1977.

Douglass, Enid H. ''Oral History,'' in David F. Trask and Robert W. Pomeroy, eds ., *The Craft of Public History: An Annotated Select Bibliography.* Westport, Conn.: Greenwood Press, 1983.

Dunaway, David K., and Willa K. Baum, eds. *Oral History: An Interdisciplinary Anthology.* Nashville: American Association for State and Local History in cooperation with the Oral History Association, 1984.

Fletcher, William. *Recording Your Family History: A Guide to Preserving Oral History* with Video Tape, Audio Tape, Suggested Topics and Questions, Interview Techniques. New York: Dodd, Mead & Co., 1987.

Frisch, Michael. *A Shared Authority: Essays on the Craft and Meaning of Oral and Public History.* Albany: State University of New York Press, 1990.

Grele, Ronald J., ed. *Envelopes of Sound: The Art of Oral History.* Revised edition. Westport, Conn.: Meckler, 1990.

Henige, David. *Oral Historiography.* New York: Longman, 1982.

Hoffman, Alice M., and Howard S. Hoffman. *Archives of Memory: A Soldier Recalls World War II.* Lexington: University Press of Kentucky, 1990.

Hoopes, James. *Oral History: An Introduction for Students.* Chapel Hill: University of North Carolina Press, 1979.

Ives, Edward D. *An Oral Historian's Work. Oral History Instructional Videotape.* Northeast Historic Film, Rt. 175, Blue Hill Falls, ME 04615.

Ives, Edward D. *The Tape-Recorded Interview: A Manual for Fieldworkers in Folklore and Oral History.* Knoxville: University of Tennessee Press, 1980.

Jeffrey, Jaclyn, and Glenace Edwall, eds. *Memory and History: Essays on Remembering and Interpreting Human Experience.* Lanham, Md.: University Press of America, 1992.

Jolly, Brad. *Videotaping Local History.* Nashville: American Association for State and Local History, 1982.

Joutard, Philippe. *Ces voix qui nous viennent du passe.* Paris: Hachette, 1983.

Labrie, Vivian. *Precis de transcription de documents d'archives orales.* Quebec: Institut Quebecois de Recherche sur la Culture, 1982.

Lanman, Barry A., and George L. Mehaffy. "Oral History in the Secondary School Classroom." Los Angeles: Oral History Association, Pamphlet No. 2, 1989.

Mercier, Laurie, and Madeline Buckendorf. *Using Oral History in Community History Projects.* Los Angeles: Oral History Association, Pamphlet No. 4, 1992.

Mishler, Elliot G. *Research Interviewing: Context and Narrative.* Cambridge: Harvard University Press, 1986.

Moss, William W. *Archives, Oral History and Oral Tradition: A RAMP Study.* Paris: UNESCO, 1986.

Moss, William W. *Oral History Program Manual.* New York: Praeger, 1974.

Nathan, Harriet. *Critical Choices in Interviews: Conduct, Use, and Research Role.* Berkeley, Calif.: Institute of Governmental Studies, 1986.

Neuenschwander, John A. "Oral History and the Law." Los Angeles: Oral History Association, Pamphlet No. 1, 1985.

Oblinger, Carl. *Interviewing the People of Pennsylvania.* Harrisburg: Pennsylvania Historical and Museum Commission, 1978.

Oral History Association. *The Oral History Review,* published twice a year; OHA Newsletter, published quarterly.

Oral History Index. Westport, Conn.: Meckler, 1990.

Portelli, Alessandro. *The Death of Luigi Trastulli and Other Stories: Form and Meaning in Oral History.* Albany: State University of New York Press, 1991.

Ritchie, Donald. *Doing Oral History.* New York: Twayne Publishers, 1995.

Sapriza, Graciela. *Historia oral e historia de vida: Aportes para una historiografia feminista.* Montevideo: Grecmu [1989].

Seminario de Historia Oral del Departamento de Historia Contemporanea de la Universidad de Barcelona. *Historia y Fuente Oral.* Published twice a year.

Shopes, Linda. *Using Oral History for a Family History Project.* Nashville: American Association for State and Local History, Technical Leaflet 123, 1980.

Sitton, Thad, et al. *Oral History: A Guide for Teachers (and Others).* Austin: University of Texas Press, 1983.

Smith, Allen, ed. *Directory of Oral History Collections.* Phoenix, Ariz.: Oryz Press, 1987.

Sommer, Barbara and Mary Kay Quinlan. *Oral History Manual.* New York: Alta Mira Press, 2002.

Stielow, Frederick J. *The Management of Oral History Sound Archives.* Westport, Conn.: Greenwood Press, 1986.

Stricklin, David, and Rebecca Sharpless, eds. *The Past Meets the Present: Essays on Oral History.* Lanham, Md.: University Press of America, 1988.

Thompson, Paul. *Oral History: The Voice of the Past.* Revised edition. New York: Oxtord University Press, 1988.

Vansina, Jan. *Oral Tradition as History.* Madison: University of Wisconsin Press, 1985.

Wood, Linda P. *Oral History Projects in Your Classroom.* Carlisle, PA: Oral History Association, 2001.

Yow, Valerie Raleigh. *Recording Oral History: A Practical Guide for Social Scientists.* Thousand Oaks, CA: Sage Publications, Inc., 1994.

Appendix C: Selected Sources

Many oral history sources are available in print form or on the World Wide Web. Included here are readers, anthologies, guides, and manuals as well as several websites and links to various oral history associations. Many of the publications have extensive bibliographies. For more information also consult your local library and the Oral History Association.

ORAL HISTORY PUBLICATIONS

Charlton, Thomas L., Lois E. Myers, and Rebecca Sharpless, eds. *Handbook of Oral History*. Lanham, MD: AltaMira Press, 2006.

Charlton, Thomas L., Lois E. Myers, and Rebecca Sharpless, eds. *History of Oral History: Foundations and Methodology*. Lanham, MD: AltaMira Press, 2007.

Dunaway, David K., and Willa K. Baum, eds. *Oral History: An Interdisciplinary Anthology,* 2nd ed. Walnut Creek, CA: AltaMira Press, 1996.

Grele, Ronald J., ed. *Envelopes of Sound: The Art of Oral History,* 2nd ed. New York, NY: Praeger, 1991.

Lanman, Barry A., and Laura M. Wendling, eds. *Preparing the Next Generation of Oral Historians: An Anthology of Oral History Education*. Lanham, MD: AltaMira Press, 2006.

MacKay, Nancy. *Curating Oral Histories: From Interview to Archives*. Walnut Creek, CA: Left Coast Press, 2006.

Neuenschwander, John A. *A Guide to Oral History and the Law*. New York, NY: Oxford University Press, 2009.

Perks, Robert, and Alistair Thomson, eds. *The Oral History Reader,* 2nd ed. New York, NY: Routledge, 2006.

Ritchie, Donald A. *Doing Oral History: A Practical Guide,* 2nd ed. New York, NY: Oxford University Press, 2003.

Ritchie, Donald A., ed. *The Oxford Handbook of Oral History*. New York, NY: Oxford University Press, forthcoming.

Thompson, Paul. *The Voice of the Past: Oral History,* 3rd ed. New York, NY: Oxford University Press, 2000.

Trimble, Charles E., Barbara W. Sommer, and Mary Kay Quinlan. *The American Indian Oral History Manual: Making Many Voices Heard*. Walnut Creek, CA: Left Coast Press, 2008.

Whitman, Glenn. *Dialogue with the Past: Engaging Students and Meeting Standards through Oral History*. Walnut Creek, CA: AltaMira Press, 2004.

Yow, Valerie Raleigh. *Recording Oral History: A Guide for the Humanities and Social Sciences,* 2nd ed. Walnut Creek, CA: AltaMira Press, 2005.

ORAL HISTORY ASSOCIATION PUBLICATIONS

Oral History and the Law, 3rd ed. John A. Neuenschwander for the Oral History Association, 2002.

Oral History Association *Evaluation Guidelines,* http://www.oralhistory.org.

Using Oral History in Community History Projects, Laurie Mercier and Madeline Buckendorf for the Oral History Association, 2007.

WEBSITES

Capturing the Living Past: An Oral History Primer. An oral history tutorial on the Nebraska State Historical Society website: http://www.nebraskahistory.org/lib-arch/research/audiovis/oral_history/index.htm.

Making Sense of Oral History. History Matters: The U.S. Survey Course on the Web: http://historymatters.gmu.edu/mse/oral.

Oral History listserver. H-Oralhist is an international network for scholars and professionals active in studies related to oral history: http://www.h-net.msu.edu/~oralhist.

Oral History: Workshop on the Web. Baylor University Institute for Oral History: http://www.baylor.edu/Oral_History/index.php?id=23560.

ORAL HISTORY ASSOCIATIONS

Oral History Association. Established in 1966, it provides professional guidance in a collegial atmosphere. Publishes the biannual *Oral History Review* (March and September), the thrice-yearly *Newsletter*, and a pamphlet series. For more information, see the website: http://www.oralhistory.org.

Michigan Oral History Association, www.h-net.org/~oralhist/moha.

Midwest Oral Historians, http://archives.library.wisc.edu/oral-history/about.html.

New England Association for Oral History, www.ucc.uconn.edu/~cohadm01/neaoh.html.

Northwest Oral History Association, c/o Idaho State Historical Society, http://www.his.state.mt.us/finduse/noha.asp.

OHMAR: Oral History in the Mid-Atlantic Region, http://www.ohmar.org.

Southwest Oral History Association, http://www.southwestoralhistory.org.

Texas Oral History Association, http://www.baylor.edu/toha/.

ORAL HISTORY ASSOCIATIONS IN OTHER COUNTRIES

Many countries have oral history associations that support the work of oral historians. Examples are the Canadian Oral History Association (http://www.canoha.ca/) and the Oral History Association of Australia (http://www.ohaa.net.au/).

INTERNATIONAL ORAL HISTORY ASSOCIATION

International Oral History Association. This is a worldwide network of oral history scholars, professionals, and researchers. For more information, see http://www.ioha.fgv.br.

Index

About the Authors

Barbara W. Sommer, an oral historian for almost thirty years, has spent her career in the field of public history, serving as historical organization director and director or codirector for numerous oral history projects. She has led oral history workshops and has presented at state, regional, and national, and international conferences. She is one of the founders of the Oral History Association of Minnesota and the Nebraska Foundation for the Preservation of Oral History, and is a longtime member of the Oral History Association, where she served as liaison to the American Association for State and Local History. She has taught oral history at the University of Nebraska–Lincoln, and Nebraska Wesleyan University. Sommer is the author of *Hard Work and a Good Deal: The Civilian Conservation Corps in Minnesota*, released by the Minnesota Historical Society Press in January 2008. With Mary Kay Quinlan, she is coauthor of *The Oral History Manual* and *The People Who Made It Work: A Centennial History of the Cushman Motor Works*, and with Quinlan and Paul Eisloeffel, she is a coauthor of *Capturing the Living Past: An Oral History Primer*, on the Nebraska Historical Society website (http://www.nebraskahistory.org/lib-arch/research/audiovis/oral_history/index.htm. 2005). She is the coauthor with Charles E. Trimble and Mary Kay Quinlan of *The American Indian Oral History Manual: Making Many Voices Heard*, released in Fall 2008. Forthcoming publications include a community oral history toolkit with Quinlan and Nancy MacKay (scheduled for release in 2012). Sommer holds a bachelor's degree from Carleton College and a master's degree in history from the University of Minnesota.

Mary Kay Quinlan, Ph.D., is an associate professor of journalism at the University of Nebraska–Lincoln (UNL), and has been editor of the Oral History Association *Newsletter* since 1993. She was a Washington correspondent for the *Omaha World-Herald* and Gannett News Service and served as president of the National Press Club. She is a longtime member of the Oral History Association and Oral History in the Mid-Atlantic Region. Quinlan has taught undergraduate and graduate journalism courses at UNL and the University of Maryland and has taught oral history at UNL and Nebraska Wesleyan University. She has presented oral history workshops at local, regional, national, and international conferences. With Barbara W. Sommer, she is coauthor of *The Oral History Manual* and *The People Who Made It Work: A Centennial History of the Cushman Motor Works*. With Sommer and Paul Eisloeffel, she is coauthor of *Capturing the Living Past: An Oral History Primer* on the Nebraska State Historical Society website. With Sommer and Charles E. Trimble, she is coauthor of *The American Indian Oral History Manual: Making Many Voices Heard*. She is also a frequent book reviewer for *The Oral History Review*. Quinlan holds a B.A. from the University of Nebraska–Lincoln, where she was a member of Phi Beta Kappa, and an M.A. and Ph.D. from the University of Maryland.